CULTURE OF THE SELFIE

SELF-REPRESENTATION IN CONTEMPORARY VISUAL CULTURE

ANA PERAICA

Theory on Demand #24
Culture of the Selfie: Self-Representation in Contemporary Visual Culture

Author: Ana Peraica
Editorial Support: Leonieke van Dipten
Copy-editing: Veena Hariharan
Cover design: Katja van Stiphout
Design: Isabella Calabretta
EPUB development: Isabella Calabretta
Publisher: Institute of Network Cultures, Amsterdam, 2017
ISBN: 978-94-92302-17-5

Contact
Institute of Network Cultures
Phone: +3120 5951865
Email: info@networkcultures.org
Web: http://www.networkcultures.org

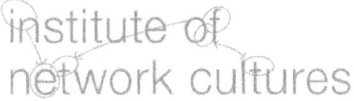

To my sister Tina.

CONTENTS

PREFACE

We don't know how to exist anymore without imagining ourselves as a picture.[1]

Although photography is not my profession, rather media art history and visual studies, I work in production of visual imagery, in the family-owned photographic studio. Not getting a tenured job in the highly corrupt country of Croatia, I have continued with the family business that I inherited from my late father and grandfather, even as professional photography as a vocation has started to disappear in the wake of a plethora of do-it-yourself (DIY) photographic practices that have emerged in recent times.[2]

Let me begin by narrating an experience in the studio before the selfie became so widely popular. Only a few years ago, I glued a sticker on our studio window, warning that photographing in our studio is not allowed. It seemed so paradoxical – forbidding photographing in a photographic studio – but at that point many tourists and passers-by recorded me while I was photographing others, just to amuse themselves. I found this practice irritating as well as humiliating towards the people coming to get their personal portraits done at our atelier. In years succeeding, in order to repel the cameras from outside, I introduced many concealing devices: curtains, flashes orientated towards the outside *et cetera*. But then suddenly this was no longer a concern, and strangely enough, it had disappeared by itself. Now, there are hundreds of tourists self-photographing daily, turning their backs onto our atelier. Reality commonly set in front of the author is now pushed into the photographically irrelevant, second plane of existence, behind his back.

Selfie as Trend

It is not only focus and perspective that has changed with selfies. It is also the quality and quantity of the images. Selfies are recorded in series and most of the shots, except the best, are erased. The reasons may lie in the insecurity of the person recording, but also in the rise of a new type of neuroticism, ridiculed by internet portals, suggesting that the APA has now officially recognized a disease named *selfitis*.[3]

Meanwhile 'selfie' was also pronounced the Word of the Year 2013 by Oxford Dictionaries. Besides reasons for nominating the word of the year for the increased frequency of its use, Oxford Dictionaries have provided its historic scenarios of development:

Selfie can actually be traced back to 2002 when it was used in an Australian online forum. The word gained momentum throughout the English-speaking world in 2013 as it evolved from a social media buzzword to mainstream shorthand for a

---

1 Amelia Jones, *Self/Image: Technology, Representation and the Contemporary Subject*, London: Routledge, Taylor and Francis, 2006, p. XVII.
2 I name these practices 'hybrid' as they can absorb all other classical photographic genres; tourist, life, landscape, body photography and self-portraiture.
3 See for example: Meghna Nair, 'Selfitis an Obsessive Compulsive Disorder of Taking too Many Selfies', *Newsgram*, 29 June 2015, http://www.newsgram.com/selfitis-an-obsessive-compulsive-disorder-of-taking-too-many-selfies/.

self-portrait photograph. Its linguistic productivity is already evident in the creation of numerous related spin-off terms showcasing particular parts of the body like *helfie* (a picture of one's hair) and *belfie* (a picture of one's posterior); a particular activity – *welfie* (workout selfie) and *drelfie* (drunken selfie), and even items of furniture – *shelfie* and *bookshelfie*.[4]

There have been many timely research projects dealing with contemporary self-photographing cultures that have developed since. One of the largest research projects surely is *Selfiecity*, a research in digital humanities led by Lev Manovich, investigating the formal style of selfies in five locations on our planet.[5] Although the book by Manovich is not yet published, there are many online sections that are a useful source for theoretical approaches to the selfie genre.[6] Besides being deeply researched from the perspective of digital humanities, selfies as online phenomenon has provoked new theoretical and practical projects. One of them, *Selfie Research Network*, curated by Theresa Senft, gathers many researchers around the topic of self-recorded network images, proposing even some courses on selfies at university levels.[7] Their daily updated Facebook page has been a great source in this research too, as well as some articles in a special issue of *International Journal of Communication* (IJOC).[8]

But is it Art?

As art historian by vocation, I am interested in the continuity of contemporary selfie culture with the tradition of self-portraiture in art. Selfies indeed lie in a direct relationship to the whole history of self-photographs, but also self-portraits and its relationship to the self and others (as described in the self-image). Many of them indeed resemble artworks of famous artists, for example the #*selfie olympics*.[9]

---

4   'The Oxford Dictionaries Word of the Year 2013', *Oxford Dictionaries*, 2013, http://blog. oxforddictionaries.com/press-releases/oxford-dictionaries-word-of-the-year-2013/.
5   Selfiecity, http://selfiecity.net/.
6   Parts of upcoming Manovich's book 'Instagram and Contemporary Image' are online, as Lev Manovich, 'Subjects and styles in Instagram Photography', Manovich, 2016, http://manovich.net/index.php/ projects/subjects-and-styles-in-instagram-photography-part-1.
7   Selfie Research Network, http://www.selfieresearchers.com/.
8   IJOC, http://ijoc.org/.
9   Selfie Olympics was launched during the times of Olympic Winter games in Sochi, in January 2014. It started introducing different hashtags, such as #*selfiegame* and #*selfieolympics* showing people in unusual positions and circumstances. Chris Lingebach, 'Selfie Olympics Take over Twitter', *Washington CBS Local*, 4 January 2014, http://washington.cbslocal.com/2014/01/04/trending-2014-selfie-olympics-take-over-twitter/.

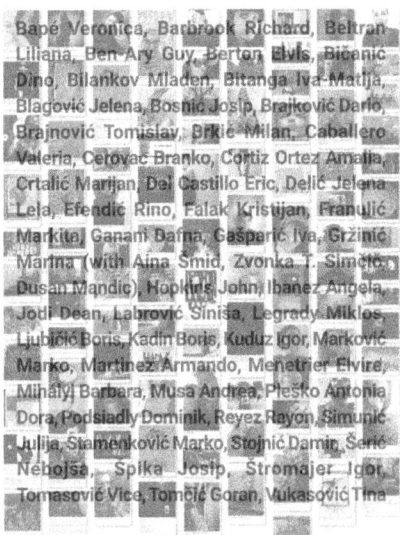

Image 1 – #whataboutyourselfie poster (design; Nikola Križanac, 2016).

To approach selfies from the perspective of art history is difficult, as self-portraiture was hardly ever a major art genre, but more a kind of art curiosity. There are hardly any anthologies of people's self-portraits.[10] The rare books on histories of self-portraiture are James Hall's deep historic overview and Amelia Jones' contemporary media historical introduction to the subject.[11] In interpretative art history, a common obstacle is connected to the mystification of the artist's relationship to the self. So, even when interested in self-portraiture, art historic sources often reflect a tendency for pseudo-psychoanalysis, attributing moods and illnesses to painters or photographers as impetus for the production of such imagery.[12] Although it is indeed a fact that reasons for self-portraying were often motivated by illness.

No wonder then that there are only few collections of early self-portraits. A rare real collection of self-portraits in the Uffizi gallery in Florence is a collection of around thousand and six hundred self-portraits, among which are ones painted by the Great Masters Rembrandt, Velázquez, Delacroix et al.[13] Currently, the collection is still expanding to include 20th century artists too. This well-chosen gallery of the most important self-portraits of the 17th and 18th centuries is still not exhaustive, as the exhibited portraits were chosen according to the authors' fame at the time. Some self-portraits can also be found in the National Portrait Gallery in London. Large numbers of these images were practice exercises in style, as artists posed

---

10 One of the first collections of self-portraits, founded in 1664, was owned by Cardinal Leopoldo de' Medici.

11 James Hall, *The Selfportrait, A Cultural History*, London: Thames and Hudson, 2014. See also: *Jones, Self/Image*.

12 Gen Doy, *Picturing the Self: Changing View on the Subject in Visual Culture*, London: I. B. Tauris, 2005.

13 Nephew of Cardinal Leopoldo de' Medici, Grand Duke Cosimo III hanged around 1600 portraits in Vasari's corridor at the Uffizi. In 1681, most of these artworks have passed revision by a curator Filippo Baldinucci, who has cut them to standard frame. See more: Uffizi, Vasari Corridor, http://www.uffizi.org/the-vasari-corridor/.

for themselves in the mirror when not being able to afford models. Because of this, many self-portraits are ephemeral, artistically irrelevant exercises. Finally, there is no museum, no archive of self-pictures of ordinary people.

On that formal level, to me as an art historian, the picture of self is iconographically impenetrable, dysfunctional, unreadable and closed, as the portrait picture of an ordinary person is not iconic at all, and it contains no general meaning to be identified. This is something artistic self-portraits and media-based selfies have in common; most of them are in an iconographical sense completely meaningless, with hardly any narrative attached to it. Moreover, in self-portraits this reference exists only vis-à-vis oneself. It is circular.

If the artists were unknown during their lifetime it is hard to assign their self-portraits to their names. It so happens that the history of art is full of self-portraits appearing as undistinguished artworks! In many cases, it is hard to prove a self-portrait is not a portrait and the other way around. Sometimes it may happen that no one knows who is represented at all. At other times a portrayed person does not resemble the image of the painter in the first place, as it has been rather a matter of self-interpretation than a direct copy of a mirror image. To connect the individual characteristics of each person; imprints of individual faces and signatures, additional guarantors either on the authorship, such as style or facial features are needed. To know who is portrayed, comparative material, visual or written, is essential. Self-portraits are doubly signed bringing the artistic style along with the artist's signature. But once this connection between names and images symbolizing the same person is established, it testifies to both style and signature better than any other genre.

And if self-portraits are not done in the style anticipated as the author's style, it is questionable if such self-portraits are more than curiosities. Containing no authentic author's insight these self-portraits somehow fail to be the real ones. For example, with media transitions and translations the authorship of the portrait is displaced. A self-portrait based on a photograph of the person made by someone else, no matter that the painting was done by the person represented, if produced after a photograph by another author, cannot fully satisfy a demand for the authorship in self-portraiture.[14]

Contrary to artistic self-portraits, produced mainly for exhibiting in art institutions, popular self-portraits and selfies are produced for completely different reasons. There are many possible personal motives, for example, producing an intimate *souvenir*, projecting a desirable image for future generations, crying out for help, or just as play. As these selfies do not become institutionalized as artistic artifacts, the question of 'are selfies made by artists art?', becomes one of the crucial points of departure. Selfies, being network-based self-portraits, are private records published in a public sphere, so they cannot be seen as fully private visual artifacts. But is the selfie a form of art if it satisfies the condition of genesis, as being produced by someone who is an artist, or representing an artist's cognitive encounter with himself or his own style? That was my other question.

---

14   This is, for example, the case of Vincent Van Gogh's self-portrait from 1886, made after a photographic
      picture. Painting a portrait of himself after the photographic picture of the author unknown to us, Van
      Gogh has pictured himself via the eyes of someone else. He has painted the way he was seen by
      someone else, in this case photographer Victor Morin.

#whataboutyourselfie

To understand differences in art production of self-portraits and selfies, I have undertaken a preliminary internet project. I had started the analysis on the topic in the field I knew best, and that is contemporary art and media art history. For these purposes, I have conceived a hashtag #whataboutyourselfie, working on different social networks (Facebook, Twitter, Google+, Youtube, Instagram…), inviting general artists to participate by uploading self-portraits and selfies using a tag #whataboutyourselfie.[15] Artists deciding to collaborate with this project were; Veronica Bape, Richard Barbrook, Guy Ben-Ary, Liliana Beltran, Dino Bičanić, Mladen Bilankov, Iva-Matija Bitanga, Elvis Berton, Jelena Blagović, Josip Bosnić, Dario Brajković, Tomislav Brajnović, Milan Brkić, Valeria Caballeroa, Branko Cerovac, Amalia Cortiz Ortez, Marijan Crtalić, Pedro Alves de Veiga, Eric Del Castillo, Pablo Del Castillo, Romina Dušić, Rino Efendić, Kristijan Falak, Markita Franulić, Dafna Ganani, Iva Gašparić, Gržinić Marina (with Aina Šmid, Zvonka T. Simčič, Dusan Mandić), John Hopkins, Angela Ibanez, Jodi Dean, Božidar Jurjević, Siniša Labrović, Miklos Legrady, Boris Ljubičić, Boris Kadin, Igor Kuduz, Marko Marković, Armando Martinez, Elvier Menetrier, Barbara Mihályi, Andrea Musa, Antonia Dora Pleško, Dominik Podsiadly, Niko Princen, Rayon Reyez, Lina Rica, Julija Simunić, Marko Stamenković, Damir Stojnić, Nebojša Šerić – Šoba, Iija Šoškić, Josip Špika, Igor Štromajer, Vice Tomasović, Goran Tomčić and Tina Vukasović.[16]

Some outcomes were more than predictable. Older artists did not respond to the call for artworks as demanded, by directly uploading images on social networks, rather they have asked a curator to choose one by herself and upload the work selected from the administrator's end, as in the classic curatorial selection for exhibition. Some authors were sending pictures rather passionately and obsessively, in a higher frequency and density, uploading multiple ones at once. Students' selfies were different from the more experimental self-portraits of their professors. Still, some new practices of framing, allowing cut-ups, and unusually high angles were introduced by younger generations. Younger generations also recorded with a direct gaze into the camera, while older authors avoided a direct self-picture, as if trying to establish some critical relationship to the concept of the self, from where a shift in audience theory became important in self-recording practices. Thus, only younger generations and media artists were sending selfies, meaning posed images recorded by hand, or selfie stick with inbuilt shutter release, and directly uploaded: while all others sent self-portraits in which they were either distancing from the camera through the use of the shutter timer, or being photographed by others in staged environments acting as if they were not posing.

Although being open to the unknown internet self-portrayers, the project had little success with them.[17] Still, it has given a ground for analyzing if there is a boundary between selfies and

---

15   #Whataboutyourselfie was a temporary web based project, www.whataboutyourselfie.info, organized by the promotion of a hashtag [#]. To participate all one had to do is to add #whataboutyourselfie to any existing image on social networks, or post a status on any of the social networks; Facebook, Twitter, Instagram, Google+, Youtube. The input from the side of organizers included adding examples of historic self-portraits while new ones were expected from the side of artists.

16   Besides them, my thanks go to the curatorial assistant Anđelko Mihanović, who has managed to follow posts on different channels, and to the rest of the team.

17   Campaign on Facebook, between 1-7 February, 2016, invited artists and students from New York, Tokyo, Sidney and London. Tokyo public has clicked 330 times on 16.151 ads released, New York 280 on 12.671. The least active were London with 265 clicks on 19.722 and Sidney with 116 on 14.839 ads. New York public was the most active in regard to the other cities. Total number of the public

self-portraits made by artists and selfies made by anyone else in the digital universe, which would be the topic of this book.

Acknowledgments

Although not specifically analyzing the results of this project in a visual sense, rather the questions and dilemmas posed by it, #whataboutyourselfie plays a part in this book's conclusions. So, I would personally like to express my gratitude, besides to all the authors participating in the project, to photographers and artists who provided me with the rights to publish their work, among which Miguel Angel Gaüeca, Joan Fontcuberta, Marta de Menezes and others. Besides, I would like to express my thanks to my students of MA in Media Art Histories (generation 2015/6) and MA in Media Art Cultures (generation 2016/7) at the Image Science Department of University of Danube in Lower Austria, who have contributed by commenting on my lectures on this particular theme.

I would like to express many thanks to my friend and publisher Geert Lovink for supporting this publication so that it did not to end up in my drawer. I would also like to thank my sister Tina Peraica, psychotherapist herself, for assisting me with literature for the therapy related section of this book, as well as to Ružica Šimunović and Janka Vukmir for assistances with other materials. Many thanks to my mum Dragica, who backed me up at the atelier when I had to do my last edits of this manuscript.

Split, 7 September 2016.

reached was 65.675 people. The number of likes has grown towards the end of the campaign period. Paid campaign ads were distributed locally, by inviting friends to like the page and event on Facebook.

INTRODUCTION

My grandfather used to make many self-portraits back when it was far more complicated to do so. Being a photographer, he had an opportunity to self-record his own life thoroughly. There are hundreds of self-portraits he self-recorded in the period from sixteen to fifty years old. The oldest one, in my knowledge, is the one taken at the Borowitz studio, where he worked as a photographer apprentice, starting at the age of six. One night, back in 1932, as recorded on the back of the photograph, he entered the studio together with his friends, with an aim to record this image for the future.

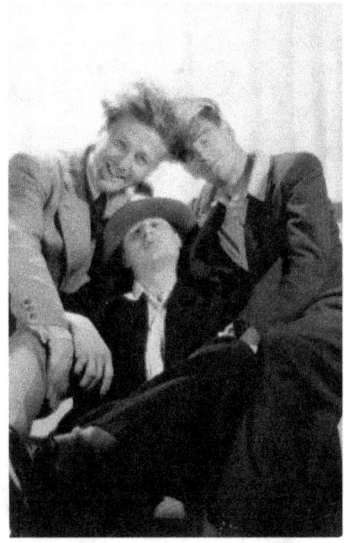

Image 2 – My grandfather's self-portrait at Borowitz' studio (Antonio Perajica, circ. 1932, family archive).

Posing like the three of them are; drunk, acting as gangsters, and mimicking movie characters, I see the picture as a projection of how they wanted to be remembered; performing 'bad guys', as wild youth who will never grow older. However, that is exactly how I knew my grandfather, as very old, only some traces of his facial features resembled the young boy recorded in the self-portrait, a youthful self that I never met.

My grandfather's practice of self-storing started in his 30s, paradoxically, during wartime. In the rigid and dangerous times of WW2 he recorded dozens of self-portraits. Contrary to his studio portrait that seemed to say, 'This is me and I was once young too', the WW2 self-portraits scream with a life urge, 'I was there and I survived.'[18] Those were intense moments; probably mixed with feelings of sadness for lost comrades, happiness for personal survival

---

18   The same life shout I recognize in the movie my grandfather filmed during WW2. At the end of the film he walks into the camera view himself, acting as Charlie Chaplin. Then, he moves away from the camera, vanishing in the distance for a second, again returns spectacularly, and finally pulls his arm to take his camera back. Yes, that was him, he claimed, the one who has recorded the whole movie.

blended with fears of battles yet to come, and maybe an anxiety of falling into amnesia immediately following the war. He shot them so as to be capable of being remembered, not just by himself, but also by others – children not yet existing. He shot them in anticipation of the gaze of upcoming generations that ought to be proud of him. That is, after all, the only final outcome a war can have; we the children and grandchildren, are proud that he fought against Nazism in the most famous battles of the South-Eastern front.

My father too recorded his self-photographs at our studio, which was by that time my grand-father's studio, leaving traces that *he was there* too. He used to leave them for his father, as his father had done for his teacher, the photographer Borowitz. At night, my father would sneak into the atelier with his friends and my mum, his girlfriend at the time, and they would record themselves. The next morning grandfather would be surprised at seeing what he developed in the darkroom.

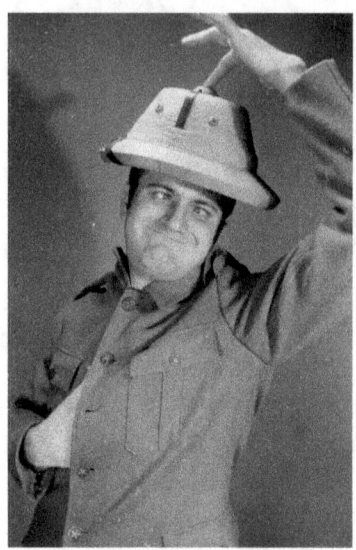

Image 3 – My father's self-portrait in studio (Dražen Perajica, around 1971, family archive).

There is a big difference between these two self-portraits. While my grandfather's portraits were made for the following generations, my father wanted to record them only as personal *communiqué* between two photographers. Whereas the intentional public of my father's photos was known, my grandfather's was not. They may have been sent to someone who might have never existed.

Selfie as Visual Paradox

Contrary to images of my father recording for his own father, or my grandfather recording for his proud grand-children, photographic theory's more famous ancestors, Roland Barthes' mother and Kendall Walton's grandmother were not recording by themselves. Still they had an intention of sending a visual message to someone not present, a message reminder in the future.[19] When seen by the intended addressee, these images provoked memories. Ancestors seem to be alive, both Barthes and Walton recognized this. But in addition to memory, I do not see only my ancestors as if being alive, but I can see them the way they actively captured themselves alive. While witnessing a live action of self-perception halted in the image, I see someone who sees himself alive, while paradoxically this person is not alive any more at the moment I look the image, so is not their self-perception.

I have conceived this book as an attempt to find historical connections and technical differences among the two genres, self-portraits and selfies, and the way they produce different discourses. In many cases, not being sure whether items are portraits or self-portraits, I have kept the original epistemic triangle of subjects-objects represented-viewers to see how the image of the self is subjectified or objectified. Self-portraits are the purest visual paradoxes that can be solved only by adding a time dimension (originally missing in two-dimensional media) to interpret a displacement between subject or the author seeing himself as an object simultaneously as the viewer sees him. So, to understand this spatial paradox, I translate a simple Lefebvrian grammatical structure into a visual schema and throughout this book draw spaces I imagine that I travel to, inside these pictures.[20] Analyzing the visual grammar of these photographs, different relationships can be found among subjects, objects, and viewers in spaces defined for and by them.

Public space is commonly defined by relationships among objects, while private space is one of residue of the subject. With viewer inhabiting one space and object – subject being in the other, I will be focused on their meeting. So, this book will be focused on space in self-portraits, shared between the person self-portraying and the viewer, and this space – merging the real space of the author and real space of the viewer, meeting in the image will be presumed as ontological, defining the self in relationship to the perceiving self, a viewer already imagined by the author, or author imagined by the viewer. Although the viewer does not form an internal consistency of the subject-object relationship, in self-portraits being looped, to analyze them comparatively with portraits, I will be introducing the viewer, as a separate epistemological agent, as a verifier of that ontological relationship – the viewer, or even – the voyeur, as the corroborator. This place I will be analyzing as the place of the Echo in the paradigmatic myth about Narcissus, but also the photographer in production of visual imagery. I will continue with the division of spaces, defining the three spaces provided in the image in general, as viewer's, object's and subject's as well as their common space; social space in photography in which viewer, object and subject communicate the message among themselves.[21]

---

19   Barthes' mother has become a paradigm of the time lost, in his *Camera Lucida*. The picture of Walton's grandfather was debated, after his own original writing, by few aestheticians. See: Roland Barthes, *Camera Lucida, Reflections on Photography*, trans. Richard Howard, New York: Hill and Wang, 2000. Kendall L. Walton, 'Transparent Pictures: On the Nature of Photographic Realism', *Critical Inquiry* 11 (1984): 246-277.

20   Henri Lefebvre, *Production of the Space*, trans. Donald Nicholson-Smith, Oxford: Wiley-Blackwell, 1992.

21   According to Lefebvre. See: Lefebvre, *Production of the Space*.

The reason this time delay and space distance appear important is because with selfies the common space is not time-delayed, but the record can be almost simultaneous to viewing. The public is set in real time to communicate with the person self-portraying. Thus, selfies simulate a common space with the viewer, space of mutual communication, while at the same time old portraits are breaking up spaces in time-sequences, as the real and simulated ones. Selfies are organized around spatial metaphors of the instant, immediate and simultaneous. Moreover, selfie constructs a hybrid space, the social space in photography, in which the timing of sociality is different than the historical one.

The key concept here will be 'perspectivality' or a capacity for suggestion of distance among agents. With perspective, a great deal of the process of objectification of self would be explained as 'setting oneself at a distance,' or objectifying. Besides, I will be distinguishing two opposite processes; subjectification of space and objectification of self, in theory commonly elaborated as perspective in visual genres and rationalization of the fear of death in visual media. Both topics, immanent to photography as its technical and media meaning, in terms of space and time descriptions, claim there is something as space-time existing even without or after us, that we agree to name: reality.[22] Transfers from self to the picture, from subject to object, I will name objectification, while rarer transfer from object to the subject, subjectification.

To answer which processes are activated when a self-portrait is shot and viewed, I obviously would need to dig much deeper in history, to analyze differences of images producing private and shared spaces. In other words, to understand selfies, it is important to distinguish mirrors and mirror-based technologies from other imaging technologies, as well as to understand their role in art history. Only with these two historical streams, is it possible to draw out differences among the three spaces present; personal space of the author as the subject, but also as the object of one's own image, and the viewer's space offered by the conversational logic of the medium. My main question would be: 'how and when did imaging technologies change from time descriptions to space descriptions, and then how did these space description technologies develop?' These technologies, I will argue, will depict the space as technologically constructed and a posteriori to its own creator, while in terms of ontological time the first and a priori to him/her, or timeless.

As objects of the self-portrait are the actual subjects of it and vice versa, the space in which they collapse is often described without a neutral reality, *res extensa*, i.e. existing without a subject which is creating it and viewer perceiving it. In this book, I will prove that disappearance of space in the images leads to a full disappearance of the space for witness and finally the reality itself.

As constructed space continues to exist without a viewer, with the contemporary paradigm of the disappearance of the viewer that actually started with the disappearance of the space for the viewer, yet another distinction will be important, and that is between descriptions of reality. I will approach two descriptions of reality; one set in front of the author, described for us via 'perspective', and the reality set behind the author's back, in which the mirror or a mirror based technology would be used either for including the reality behind the back, or to actually exclude it. Although it sounds terrifying, this reality set behind the author's back

---

22   Here I will continue defining the ontology of the image as I have previously done in my thesis
      Photography as Evidence. See: Ana Peraica *Fotografija kao dokaz*, PhD diss., Faculty of Humanist and
      Social Sciences, University of Rijeka, Rijeka/Croatia, 2010.

will prove useful in situations where a fear of direct confrontation, or laying out in perspective, overwhelms the visuals – as for example in funeral selfies and selfies with cadavers.

Book Overview

To be able to analyze the separation of the self-portrait from the portrait genre and furthermore selfie from the self-portrait, in the first chapter, I go over these slightly dissonant histories; history of self-observation via the history of the mirror and lenses, and the history of self-recording as media history. In the second chapter, I lay out the history of space in self-portraiture as visual studies history, elaborating on positions of subjects, objects and viewers in terms of the history of mirrors, lenses, cameras and perspective, while hoping that this triangulation will not resonate as overly Hegelian or orthodox. In the third chapter, I go back to the classical myth of Narcissus, a myth undoubtedly about self-reflection, though, not about self-imaging. As Narcissus does not need anyone else, excluding viewers from his universe, and withdrawing into his own reflection, the strategy of dematerialization, withdrawing into one's own image will be the key focus. In the fourth chapter, I will focus on the role of the viewer, or the mythical Echo and the connotations of solipsism, but also of self-transference, antisocial and social elements of self-portraiture, and the selfie as a cry for help. Here the process of subjectification of the object will be the central theme, asking for enhanced viewer's participation. The fifth chapter will be dedicated to the sort of images that control reality 'behind the back'; pictures of the dead in self-portraiture, in which the process of objectification of the body, succeeded with a rationalization of fear, will be highlighted. In the sixth chapter, I will shortly focus on mirror-based technologies, laying out definitions of space emerging with the new culture of the selfie. And finally, in the conclusion, I will provide the analysis of a selfie along with a self-portrait using concepts clarified in previous chapters, closing with a redefinition of models of power based on surveillance and self-exposure.

As my main goal would be to describe the paradigm shifts in space description, besides its travel from front to back of the subject, I will conclude with the final analysis of differences of the Medieval, Modern and post-real cognition of self and reality, in which different orga-nizations between subject and reality existed. Contemporary selfies, contrary to the Modern depiction of self as the only content of the image, do show reality. Still, this reality, contrary to the place of Mantegna in his *Christ in Temple*, or Van Eyck's mirror, is not set in front of the author, but, as I already mentioned, behind his back, describing the author himself as the object, not the subject. This objectification and mediatization of reality cannot but draw to a conclusion; it might have been we have arrived at the stage the reality cannot be expe-rienced and learned directly, but only as mediated and reflected, similarly as the self cannot be subjectified.

I. HISTORIES OF SELF-OBSERVATION

Three micro histories intertwine in the contemporary selfie phenomenon; the history of the mirror in which the subject is posing, history of deposing this image in a storage medium, and the history of representation constructed within the medium; connecting it again with the outside world of the viewer who in turn reconstructs the original performative act of posing. In short, simultaneous histories of the object posing, subject viewing, and audience reconstructing the view are often set in this paradoxical rebus of subject, object, and viewer, in which the subject is at the same time an object, often also taking the place of the viewer.

History of Self-Observing

In rewinding a history of posing in front of the mirror, it is common to refer to the phenomenon of 'narcissist delight'. Narcissist delight is probably as old as self-awareness, and it is indeed hard to map its first appearance in the history of reception. What appears easier to do is to time-map dates of different types of mirror productions as both archaeological and anthropological objects, relating them to the most common imaging practices.

The oldest mirrors were found in Anatolia, around 4000 BC. These objects, later used by Romans and pre-Columbian Mexicans, were hardly transparent. They were black and made out of volcanic materials, such as obsidian. Egyptians, Etruscans, and Greeks made mirrors lighter using silver, copper and tin. Many of them were found in graves, evidently having functions related to faith in afterlife, a practice that continues even today in some contemporary cultures.[23] Greeks even attributed the origin of the mirror to God Hephaestus who gave his wife presents as jewels and mirrors.[24] During the Medieval ages, mirrors were small and dark, and actually dangerous as they contained, according to Sara Schechner, poisons such as arsenic, besides silver, wine sediments or even tartar, antimony, brass, borax and English pewter.[25] Perhaps for that reason they were seen as Devil's instruments, and undeniable proof that the women who used them were engaged in witchcraft.[26]

Because of the difficult manual labor of producing glass in ancient times, mirrors were rare and pricey, which made them luxury objects inaccessible to ordinary people. This means the unimaginable for us in contemporary civilizations; women groomed themselves and men shaved their beards without ever having any possibility of seeing themselves! Only in the 15th century, when glass manufacture was initiated on a large scale, using soda, lime, and silica or sand silicates, that it became easier to manufacture larger series of mirrors. Despite mechanization of production, their price remained high as they were controlled and protected by secret guilds. Recipes for glass production were clandestine, and Bohemian manufacturers kept them carefully hidden from the Venetians. Eventually they managed to crack the

23 Some Balkan practices cover up the mirror in the house when someone dies, as death could show his face from it.
24 Roman parallel of the myth is retold through the character of Vulcan.
25 Sara J. Schechner, 'Between Knowing and Doing: Mirrors and Their Imperfections in the Renaissance', *Early Science and Medicine* 10.2, (2005): 137-162.
26 Beatrice de Planissoles was one of them, accused for a variety of 'objects, strongly suggestive of having been used by her to cast evil spells' among which was a mirror and knife.

secret code and perfected the method of crystal glass, purifying the mirror layout. This fully displaced its production to the European south and initiated the production of glass mirrors on the island Murano, that continues to be a center of glass production even today. Once the Venetian recipe was implemented and upgraded by the Saint Gobain Company, founded in 1665 in France, initiating mass production, prices of mirrors finally started falling.[27] It was only then that workers and peasants afforded to see what they really looked like, along with which grooming practices and people's appearance also began to change.

Shapes were very important for the quality of the mirror. Initially, glasses were concave, convex glasses did not appear until around 1589.[28] Around that time mirrors become larger and as such a desirable luxury, still, only the elite could possess them. Filling large places as famous Chamber of Mirrors of Henri I and Catherine de' Medici, Hall of Mirrors in Versailles, built by Charles le Brun, or Lafayette by Louis XIV, mirrors were exposed on large quantity, as a sign of wealth and luxury.

Shapes of mirrors also influenced the development of visual culture and each of its upgrades has changed the history of art and its findings. Popular hyper-realist artist David Hockney and physicist Charles M. Falco have attempted to prove that the realism of Renaissance owes to the invention of the convex mirror.[29] Late Renaissance and Baroque artists, such as Michelangelo Merisi da Caravaggio, according to the same authors, used convex shapes more frequently, which according to Erwin Panofsky is more natural to the eye as it corresponds to the retinal image.[30] Hockney and Falco later broadened their thesis with proofs that even late medieval artists such as Flemish painters Jan Van Eyck and Robert Campin, used optical devices, demonstrating the method on Jan Van Eyck's *Giovanni Arnolfini and His Wife* (1434) and *Portrait of Cardinal Niccolo Albergati*, in first of which the artist's self-portrait appeared in a concave mirror.[31] Falco also measured specific types of technologies as well their distortions, proving that artists of Romanticism, such as Jean-Auguste Dominique Ingres, used optical devices to produce their painterly work. These assumptions became known as the Hockney-Falco thesis and were widely criticized, raising a number of counter-arguments from the science of optics, and the history of science.[32]

---

27   For history of the company, see: Saint-Gobain, https://www.saint-gobain.com/en/group/our-history.
28   Schechner, *Between Knowing and Doing*.
29   David Hockney and Charles M. Falco, 'Optical insight into Renaissance Art', *Optics & Photonics News* 11.7, (2000): 52-59.
30   Erwin Panofsky, *Perspective as Symbolic Form*, trans. Christopher S. Wood, New York: Zone Books, 1991 (1927).
31   Ibid.
32   So, for example, physicians such as David G. Stork whose calculations showed physical distortions in their thesis, while historians of science such as Sara Schechner (2009), proved technologies as concave mirrors were not yet manufactured at the moment paintings were done. Schechner claims there is no evidence that convex mirrors were produced before XVI century, when it is Maurolycus and della Porta mention them firstly. Schechner, *Between Knowing and Doing*. Still, Criminisi and others prove the mirror could have also been even by a convex mirror. Antonio Criminisi, Martin Kemp and Sing B. Kang, 'Reflections of Reality in Jan van Eyck and Robert Campin', *Historical Methods: A Journal of Quantitative and Interdisciplinary History* 37.3 (2004).

From Camera Obscura Selfie to the Digital Selfie

Lonely dreamers may have invented modern technologies, based on lenses and/or mirrors, such as camera obscura and camera lucida, but their histories coincided with that of elites, who were their first consumers. It is undeniable that photography as technology was a product of the painters' imagination. It is hard to prove if camera obscura, or its descendants, such as camera obscura were ever used to record self-portraits. And if they were, due to the complexity of the technology, these cases would surely be rare ones. Only with the successor of the camera obscura – the photo camera – photographic technology has enabled the arrival of self-portraits.

However, producing self-portraits with photographic equipment was extremely difficult until the development of the shutter release and self-timer device, patented in 1918. The timer was implemented into photographic cameras only by the 20s, allowing automatic self-portraying possibilities. A device for a delayed action at the beginning pneumatic, delayed shutter closure for a half of a second up to three minutes, leaving enough time to run into a pre-prepared scene. Later the automatic camera allowed even non-professionals to engage in such self-recording. Agfa's Optima, introduced in 1959 was the first such model enhancing self-imaging, soon followed by Kodak's 1963 Instamatic.

Even with growing numbers of users, the problem of assistance in processing pictures remained. Despite becoming easier to arrange the scene to self-record, the process of developing photographs from 35mm or, even worse, middle size formats, was a complicated one, commonly handled by professional labs, where someone would actually see the photographs printed before the author who has taken them. These potential someone-else-could-see photographs often led to self-censorship. The exception was the Polaroid process, invented in 1947, that a number of artists used at the time, in which the author could finish the photographic processing oneself.[33] Still, the picture's material non-durability made it unpopular after the 70s when a bad chemical stabilization of Polaroid pictures became clear, as images simply vanished. It took decades until its digital replacement was invented.[34]

In the 90s the first digital camera was invented, and its development paved the way for eliminating professionals out of the photographic chain. This process was completed with the advent of mobile-phone technology that was always immediately at hand and could be used by any one at any moment, contrary to static, immobile and demanding standard photographic equipment. The first camera-phone was sold in Japan around the turn of the century, when the technology of digital recording was already a decade old. In 2012 camera-phones started competing with professional digital technology, introducing 42 million pixels on semi-professional, DX-sensor. After thousands of years, it was only with mobile phone technology, that for the first time all social classes had a tool for self-reflection, self-presentation, and self-promotion.

---

33   See for example; Peter Buse, *The Camera does the rest*, Chicago: University of Chicago Press, 2016.
34   Even then mirrors continued to be interesting. For example, artists Dan Graham, who constructed environments, such as *Present, continuous past* (1974) or performances like *Audience Mirror* (1975).

History of Self-Presentation[35]

Self-presentation is, paradoxically, much older than its technology, relying on the classical media of self-storage, and having no mirroring capacities. One of the first known self-presentations in art dates back to the sculptor of Egyptian pharaoh Akhenaten, Bak, who has left a portrait of himself and his wife standing in one of the sculptural plastics in the rulers' tomb.[36] Pliny the Elder has mentioned two self-portraits in Greek times; the self-portrait of Theodorus, representing himself in a bronze miniature in a chariot, and Iaia of Cyzicus.[37] Iaia was known as a portraitist, but she also made some self-portraits.[38] In Greece, with the first appearance of the author's signature, artists could be traced and followed. Though, even with the rise of self-awareness, self-portraiture was not a genuine genre, nor was it generally acceptable. James Hall mentions a case of imprisonment of sculptor Phidias who dared to include his self-representation in the decoration on the statue of Athena.[39]

Owing to iconoclastic tendencies in all representations, self-representation including that of the self-portraits of Christ in the Middle Ages, were believed to be directly imprinted into the image, as on the Veronica's robes, laid in front of a tortured Christ on his way to Golgotha, as well as King Abgar of Edessa's Mandylion. Even when painted, medieval portraits of Christ were believed to be made with no awareness from the artist, thus as being direct self-portraits of divinities [Gr. *Acheiropoieton*]. During these times, when it was almost forbidden to self-represent, many scribes secretly imprinted their own self-portraits in miniatures. Some of them like St Dunstan and Hildebertus, wrapped their miniature pictures inside capital letters of manuscript chapters.

Around 1500 a new ideology, emancipating humans from God, came into focus. Centering the measure of the universe around the human rather than God, paradigmatically visible in Leonardo's drawing of the measure of the human, the human-creator has discovered his inner self as reality coexisting and relating to the outside one. In the first historiographies, self-portraits started reappearing on a large scale.[40] Court painters such as Albrecht Dürer, Andrea Mantegna, Adam Kraft, Pietro Perugino, Leonardo da Vinci, Sofonisba Anguissola, but also Rembrandt van Rijn, used self-portraits as proofs of their existence, and more importantly as tools of self-gratification, accompanying their new social roles as courtiers. Many of these self-portraits were commissioned to famous artists but passed on to their pupils to fill the growing market demands for them. Rembrandt was one of these artists whose self-portraits were occasionally painted by others, his pupils.[41]

---

35 Parts of this chapter were published as Ana Peraica, 'Selfie as Paradigm of Cultural Change' Ideas and paradigms of cultural change Conference, Samara Scientific Centre Samara Society for Cultural Studies, 22-23 May 2014.

36 Bak, *Self-portrait With his Wife, Taheri* (c.1353-1336 BC), stone, Quartzite, Egyptian Museum, Berlin.

37 Theodorus of Samos: *Selfportrait*, bronze (lost). Pliny refers to it as miracle similarity [Lat.'*similitudo mirabilis*'].

38 Iaia of Cyzicus, known as Marcia, referred in Boccaccio after Pliny: Iaia was a female painter from Cyzicus, and was active in Rome c. 80 BC. She was famous for a self-portrait and for her portraits of women. The miniature depicts her watching herself in a circular mirror in order to reproduce her own portraits on a canvas. Giovanni Boccaccio, *Des Claires et Nobles Femmes*, trans. by Laurent de Premierfait, Paris: Bibliothèque Nationale de France, 1402.

39 Hall, *The Selfportrait*.

40 i.e. Vasari, *The Lives of the Artist*.

41 An amazing way the originals were distinguished from non-allographic paintings appeared in small asymmetries on which the artist would focus while analyzing himself in the mirror. Pupils were fulfilling

Besides Rembrandt, Albrecht Dürer, who fully documented his own aging, processing many changes in the relationship to self, has painted the largest number of self-portraits. Dürer started self-portraying at the age of fourteen, convinced of his own classical beauty that he later used as the paradigmatic image of Christ. Rembrandt, on the contrary, followed his own emotional life, that led him to look like Methuselah at the age of only sixty-two.[42]

Alla Sfera and Allo Specchio: From Renaissance Self to Post-Modern Self

Another historical condition that influenced development of the Renaissance self-portrait was the advancement of the shape of glass mirrors. Giorgio Vasari, at the time, distinguished productions between two types of self-portraits. First, those made in a convex mirror [Ita. *alla sfera*] and second made in flat glass [Ita. *allo specchio*].[43]

Mannerism itself was influenced by the commercialization and availability of mirrors and other optical devices being collected in 'cabinets of curiosities'. As the production of mirrors had become larger, more and more frequently mirrors had become the occupation of artists since the times of Mannerism. The most interesting case is the self-portrait of Girolamo Francesco Maria Mazzola known as Parmigianino (1524), produced in the style of high Mannerism, and announcing a Modernistic relationship to the self. His *Self-portrait in a Mirror* uncovers the value in disproportion to the universe itself, in which the artist is becoming more important, thus also physically larger than he would ever be in ordinary Renaissance perspective, based on simple orthogonal Euclidian geometry.[44] The physical object of the mirror, once an object of luxury, becomes a commercial one in the late 16th century and that is when a larger number of artists started painting their self-appearance.

Yet another revolution was introduced with the invention of photographic technologies, also called 'mirror with a memory'.[45] The first photographic self-portrait recorded and also one of the first stabilized light reflections was Hippolyte Bayard's *Self-portrait as a Drawn Man* (1887), representing a dead-looking person, but signed and claimed to be a self-representation of the author.[46] This

---

the task much better as they would not correct small errors. Ernst van de Wetering, *A Corpus of Rembrandt Paintings IV*, Dordrecht: Springer, 2005.

42   John Berger in the video Embrace says he looked older than people in his own time, mentioning drinking problems. John Berger, 'Embrace', https://www.youtube.com/watch?v=Obt2nSQ2Ud0.

43   Giorgio Vasari, *The Lives of the Artist*, Oxford University Press, 1991 (c1550). Among artists working with mirrors, he describes different techniques used by Cimabue, Luca della Robbia, Masaccio, Alberti, Fra Filippo Lippi, Domenico Ghirlandaio, Da Vinci, Giorgione and Raphael.

44   Deformation of a convex mirror announces modern non-Euclidian geometry, producing the overall roundness of the image, in a manner of relativist physics of early 20th century.

45   Oliver Wendell Holmes named photography. Mirrors indeed are used in photographic reflection technology to invert image in a fixed or moving position inside the SLR camera. Still, there are numerous differences between the mirror and the photography: unlike the mirror, the photographic image is able to move, so anyone else can see it, as the photographic image is fixed. And moreover, the photographic image can show only one image in countless number of copies while a mirror can show countless number of images, still in a single copy only. From there, of course, there is a difference of human relationships with the mirror and with the photograph, especially when it portrays someone else.

46   *The Portrait of Self as a Drawn Man* was a three dimensional artifact including, besides its foreground, also the paper's background as an integral part. On the foreground, Bayard has recorded himself acting

self-portrait contained an original sophist paradox of a 'Liar' written on the backside of the positive paper print that said:

> The corpse which you see here is that of M. Bayard, inventor of the process that has just been shown to you. As far as I know this indefatigable experimenter has been occupied for about three years with his discovery. The Government, which has been only too generous to Monsieur Daguerre, has said it can do nothing for Monsieur Bayard, and the poor wretch has drowned himself. Oh the vagaries of human life...! [47]

Bayard immediately started a trend of self-dramatization in photography, which marks the early implementation of the photographic medium in the genre of self-portraiture. 19th century simulations, in their early competition with painting, were drawn to this dramatic portrait style. Perhaps due to the impossibility of recognizing if the picture is a portrait or a self-portrait, early self-photography literally suffered the allegorization of the self. Meanings of images were constructed also by the proliferation of symbols or *insignias* held in arms, and excessive hand gestures inbuilt into the frame of the 'American cut' or full figure. Two photographic self-portraits were found in this manner: Jean-Gabriel Eynard daguerreotypist *Self-Portrait with a Daguerreotype of Geneva (circa* 1847) and a picture taken by an unknown photographer named *Portrait of Unidentified Daguerreotypist* (1845).[48] In both pictures, photographers have presented themselves with medieval type of sign based attributes [Lat. *insignia*], the first one with the radio, while the other with daguerreotype products. Other authors were inventive; dressing, and acting in allegorical type of narratives, as shown in the exhibition *Self-Portrait, the Photographer's Persona.*[49]

Not all the self-portraits, however, were grounded in self-promotion. Moralizing in his pictures, Oscar Gustave Rejlander, for example, used his own body as a carrier of meanings in more complex, symbolically loaded narratives. He posed himself in staged historical live tables [Fr. *tableaux vivants*], that he has named 'combination prints'. In *On the Expression of the Emotions in Man and Animals* (1872), based on thoughts of Charles Darwin's book of the same title, he posed alone, while in *Happy Days* (1872) his wife joined him.[50] Similarly, other famous photographers at the turn of the century, Gaspard-Félix Tournachon aka Nadar and latter Edward Steichen, made many playful self-portraits, changing environments as reality backgrounds.[51]

---

as a corpse in a staged scene, while the background included text claiming he had just deceased. But, it is not possible that Bayard, the photographer, is at the same time recording the photograph, while being ultimately lifeless, ending up constructing a visual paradox, similarly to Magritte's impossible portrait of Mr. Jones. A paradox constructed between the image and the text on the backside reminds of the paradox of a liar, that says: 'Everything I say is false.' In analogy, Bayard's paradox claims that: (1) the author has to be alive to record this photograph. Thus, (2) he cannot be dead as stated on the photograph's background. So, (1+2), either it is not Bayard, or if it is – Bayard is dead (NOT 1.). As it is completely impossible for Bayard to be dead and alive at the same time, it is either the photograph that is lying or the text.

47   The J. Paul Getty Museum, http://www.getty.edu/art/collection/artists/1840/hippolyte-bayard-french-1801-1887/.

48   Daguerreotype, hand-colored, 8.3 x 7 cm, The J. Paul Getty Museum, Los Angeles.

49   Susan Kismaric, 'Self-Portrait: The Photographer's Persona, 1840-1985, *MoMA*, 37 (Autumn, 1985): 5.

50   Oscar Gustav Rejlander, *Happy Days* (c. 1872), The Royal Photographic Society Collection, National Media Museum.

51   John Hannavy, *Encyclopedia of Nineteenth-Century Photography*, New York and London: Routledge, 2008.

These portraits were however merely physiognomic, rather than attempting to show any psychological features. A rare example of psychologization of the self-portrait developed in the work of Margaret Cameron. On a *Self-portrait* from 1863, a skinny face framed by a black scarf, diving out to the surface from a deepest, blackest darkness, with eyes looking downwards, as in a prayer, Cameron appears as a nun, an ascetic woman radiating with self-sufficiency in her solitude.

The real self-portraits, in terms of depiction of the self that was not based on performance, evolved only in the Pre-modern period. Dualistic conception of the world, present in such portraits and self-portraits put an accent on the body, which was not subjectivized, resonating with the impossibility of presenting a soul, or subjectivity. Subjectivity, namely, appeared as a side effect, an epiphenomenon, an ephemeral consequence of an intrinsically physical chain of events. This binarism was further emphasized with new born symptoms of exhibitionism and accompanying voyeurism, provoked by the advancement of the new, automatic and unmanned, photographic equipment.

Around 1900, photographic self-portraits in the mirror started appearing.[52] Turn to the inner self in self-imaging was influenced by Modernist painters, whose work appeared synchronous with the rise of Freudian psychoanalysis, influencing Modern styles, especially Impressionism, Expressionism, and Surrealism.[53] These styles were concentrated on inner experience; fluid feelings were woven into paintings referring to sensations of optical phenomena, conscious emotions, or unknown subconscious ones.[54] Modern self-portraits thus had much to do with Freudian psychoanalysis, and its attempts to reach a 'true self' that was single, static, and stable.

Photographers of the era, contrary to painters, used self-portraits to play with self-images, pushed by the fact that photographs could be edited, unlike mirrors. They approached themselves in different ways; capturing a sensation or temporary mood, playing with grimaces, or even emancipated performances, but also rationally constructing a completely new identity. So, Egon Schiele made a number of photographic self-portraits in which the formal visual appearance he exercised were gestures similar to the performativity of contemporary selfie producers. His self-portraits commonly included his arms and hands inside the portrait as well as different distorted faces. Also, he gazed directly into the camera, using it simultaneously as a tool of narcissistic delight but also of communication to the public.[55]

---

52   Ruth Styles, 'Portrait of a woman recorded around 1800', *Daily Mail*, 19 November 2013, http://www. dailymail.co.uk/femail/article-2509952/Black-white-selfies-dating-1800s-shed-light-history-self-portrait. html.
53   Today one of the most analyzed artists of this era is Paul Cezanne, whose portraits are considered ideal reflection of a psychoanalytical mirror-stage, both at the physical level of the implementation of optic devices and the metaphoric level of presentation. Doublings of Cezanne portraits, already emphasized by Silverman, present two parallel moments of self-displaying visibility; one is orientated to the image of the self, while the other to the appearance of the painting.
54   Hugh J. Silverman, 'Cezanne's Mirror Phase' in *The Merleau-Ponty Aesthetics Reader: Philosophy and Painting*, Galen A. Johnson (ed), Evanston: Northwestern University Press, 1993.
55   There are many resources for different gestures, which are considered desirable by selfie-producers, such as signs of victory or boredom, but also different vulgar expressions that can be achieved with assistance of one hand only, as the other one is preoccupied with the process of recording. As in the old theatre of pantomime the speechless speech to the camera becomes a communication with the public.

Photographic split of *personae* by the use of multiple exposures are present, for example, in Marcel Duchamp and Umberto Boccioni's portraits by an unknown artist, dated 1917 and 1907, both displaying multiple pictures of a single person gathered around the table, as if chatting to himself. Futurists went even further, as Fortunato Depero who employed photo technology to alternate his own body image, or to describe his own vision of self in a metaphorical way, distorting it, for example, by multiple or slow exposures. Distortions reached a peak in the work of Hungarian artist André Kertész, who used, besides photographic techniques, different anamorphic optical devices, constructing a mannerist reality.

Characteristic experiments of Modernism were also focused on doubling of identity and identity crossing. These Modernist self-portraits engaged commonly in gender crossing, yet produced consistent selves. Parallel to using pseudonyms and alter-egos, Duchamp, dressed as a woman in a portrait entitled *Rose Sélavy*; Man Ray appeared as a lady in his self-portrait (1935); El Lissitzky in a masque of Wanda Wulz in his own self-portrait (1932) Claude Cahun, the only woman cross-dresser, dressed as a man. Experimenting with formal aspects of self-projection, expanding their roles of self towards the outside and out of one's own borders, rather than investigating or interrogating a personal recording, these self-portraits engaged in something that can be named 'photographic personality disorder', if a parallel can be drawn to a diagnosis of multiple personality disorder.[56]

One of the most interesting self-portraits from the first half of the 20th century, which can be seen in relationship to contemporary selfie culture, is the self-portrait of Umbo, or Otto Umbehr, depicting himself lying naked on the beach. What is so contemporary about Umbo's portrait is the closure of space. The artist is self-recording; his arms fill the immediate space with the photographic camera, which gazes directly onto him, eye to the eye. We as viewers, are not positioned behind the camera, but in front of it, squeezed in a small place left between Umbo's hairy chests and his, obviously, Leica camera. We see what he does not see by himself, but he wants us to see; himself as an erotic object laying down in front of us, on the blanket, under the sun.

Postmodern Self-Obsession

'Subjectivity-as-such' enters the field of analysis only with postmodern photography, concentrated on timely theoretical and political themes, rather than mere visual designs. A new self-centered universe is brought to the front by defining the limits of one's nation, gender or skin color. 'I' becomes a tool for explanation, but also the obsession with the subject-theme, centered on the concept of the mirror-stage introduced by Jacques Lacan.[57] But, most importantly, it is the postmodern reading of Lacan's distinction between the view and the gaze that is relevant to the analysis.[58]

The 'Postmodern Turn,' as it was named, is marked by the analysis of the fragmentation and instability of the self, or to paraphrase; dynamic self, based on mutual processes of deconstructions and temporary reconstructions, contrary to the Modern ideal of the stable and consistent self. The reason lays in the more complex relationship to the self,

---

Also referred to as Dissociative Identity Disorder (DID).

57 Jacques Lacan, *Mirror Stage*, Lecture at Fourteenth International Psychoanalytical Congress at Marienbad, 1936.

58 Paraphrased in a more Lacanian way; what defines me – is the gaze from the outside. Ibid.

now defined via a Postmodern theory that distinguishes person from personality, self from subject, or portrait from mood.

In line with historical developments of the writing from the 'first person,' or 'I', influenced by authors such as Roland Barthes, Jacques Derrida, or Michel Foucault, self-portraits gain an important place among other artistic genres. Notable conceptual authors self-recording in narcissistic delight are Lee Friedlander, Lucas Samaras, John Coplans, and Chuck Close, to name a few.

Feminist photography was built on the stable basis of self-portraits of Cahun, but also of Margaret Bourke-White, Lotte Jacobi, Germaine Mill, Kate Matthews and Ilse Bing, also indicating their 'male', technologically emancipated and advanced side of being as a photographer/ cameraman, self-recording with their own cameras in hands, as if to show that cameras are their own, personal, machines. Latter, feminist photography commonly depicted an under-represented, middle-aged woman, being an antipode to the image of woman in marketing, commonly young and performing according to the desiring male gaze.[59] By developing a critique of the society with the implementation or, better to say, reconstruction of the self, feminism widened a set of motifs for the production of self-portraits in art history.[60] Authors such as Cindy Sherman, Julia Scher, or Merry Alpern have explored a thin line stretched between the surveillance society and the exhibition of feminist issues.[61] They managed to separate the self to be able to analyze themselves rationally and to objectify, rather than only performing and playing some invented persona as with the artists of the Modern.

While Modern self-portraits approached this possibility of narrative by producing alternative modes of identities, illustrating hypothetic lives and parallel times of fabricated personal narratives in between real history and histrionics, on the other hand postmodern concepts of identity have shown inconsistencies on the time axis, worm-holes, and errors, in which the central point was rather a confusion of personal and public time. In Postmodernity, separation of self reaches polyvalent logics of identity, suggested by Nancy.[62] The first-person plural differentiates the capital 'Other' from the 'other' in small case, redefining the difference between the two in terms of againstness and communication. The space suddenly came strictly divided between me, who stays undefined, and the capital Other fully defined by power, and serving to define the self. Or, as Christopher Lasch affirmed, it distinguishs between the Pre-Modern and Modern self, becoming a difference in the action, admiration, and fame of Modernism, in contrast to power and glamour of postmodernism.[63]

Besides capturing changes in one's own personal states, personal identity remained in focus. Self-invention, not just moods, but the invention of the whole character, a persona, remained a challenge as in the works of Sherman or Yasumasa Morimura. There is even a large difference between role-playing in their photography, for example in Sherman and Morimura's references to classical paintings. While Sherman is not taking finite characters, such as known persons,

---

59   Ina Loewenberg, 'Reflections on Self-Portraiture in Photography', *Feminist Studies* 25.2 (1999): 398-408.

60   Also, one may speak of the destruction of the self in terms of the abject.

61   Sandra S. Phillips and Simon Baker, *Exposed: Voyeurism, Surveillance, and the Camera Since 1870*, New Haven and Connecticut: Yale University Press, 2010.

62   Jean Luc Nancy, *Being Singular Plural*, Broadway: Stanford University Press, 2000.

63   Christopher Lasch, *The Culture of Narcissism, American Life in an Age of Diminishing Expectations*, New York and London: W. W. Norton & Company, 1991 (1979).

but constructs deliberately, approximately from historic sources, providing fake evidence to history, Morimura is using historically prepared personae in his masquerades.[64] The same drive, to set and infiltrate the media producing celebrities, rather than narrations, such as magazines, TV, calls the selfie generation on experimenting even new forms.[65]

Based on the idea that the strict appearance does not provide sufficient reasons to distinguish if one image is a portrait or a self-portrait, many contemporary artworks were produced. For example, self-portraits by Sherman claimed to be actual portraits. Sherman has claimed, contrary to Bayard, that although she had recorded herself in most of her photographic works, she was not recording her self-portraits as she appeared always as-someone-else. Experiencing the sense of being 'out of her own skin' while recording, she was not connected to herself.[66] There is, indeed, no direct relationship of Sherman-photographer and Sherman-model, and at the same time the only relationship between Bayard and a self being portrayed, we know exists in a written text at the back of the picture left by Bayard (described above), so in both cases there is no guarantee as to who is the author of the picture. Thus, it seems plausible to claim that there is no self-portrait but only an action of self-portraying, in which there is no place for the viewer, either.[67]

Mass availability of equipment initiated another revolution within the photographic medium, in the 80s as photographers did not have to be professionals to master the whole process of image production anymore. While artworks of feminist artists strived to provoke a judgmental gaze, another type of art, a self-therapeutic one that asks for empathy and fully denies the narcissistic idea behind self-portraiture, reintroduced the empathic Echo into the discourse of self-reflection.

Photography, as a medium, had managed to show the hidden, oppressed, and the traumatic in reality itself, becoming a proper technology of embodiment.[68] Besides in photography, post-

---

64   In photographic self-portraiture, the space of the public, commonly though not necessary, falls in the space of the photographic equipment, through which lenses we are seeing the image. Photo-camera is our eyes and, depending on the position, it can also depict the view of the person self-portraying, providing us multiple gazes. Still, in artworks done in direct reference to some other ones, this gaze is quoted, referred to another piece and the audience should be able to read out different layers of reality. Such is the case of re-enactments of Sherman's famous *Untitled stills* by Aneta Grzeszykowska or re-reinterpretations by the same images by James Franco, which then become transvestite pieces, or Morimura's re-enactments of famous paintings. A serial of quotes transfers the original image of the audience into a space of imaging, in which a recall of classics quoted is done.

65   Although completely different, as among paying a tribute, dedicating a *hommage* and directly referring, works of Sherman and Morimura evoke Jameson's sense of postmodernity. In all the cases being literary, classical artistic references to *personae* are based on knowledge of history, on the contrary of selfies in which characters are limited to popular references as living stars and starlets, as Kim Kardashian. In both, a *pastiche*, or a parody, displaces the original scene with quoted one, complicating its spacial descriptions, but also fully migrating into the other.

66   According to a materialistic explanation of the self, it is very problematic if she keeps being the same referent in visual continuity of photography or she indeed dies and rebirths, physically, to host a new identity.

67   Jay concludes there is no place for the viewer in anti-ocularcentric works of Sherman, Burgin and Kelly from 1993. Martin Jay, *Downcast Eyes, The Denigration of Vision in Twentieth-century French Thought*, Berkeley: University of California Press, 1994.

68   Amelia Jones, 'The "Eternal Return" Self-Portrait Photography as a Technology of Embodiment', *Signs* 27.4 (2002): 947-978.

modern self-separation and segregation were also explored in the medium of video, especially in artworks in which artists are directly confronting the screen, sometimes literally pressing their faces onto the camera or the glass, as in Paul McCarthy's *Screen* (1972/4), Hannah Wilke's *Gesture II* (1974/6), Lynda Benglis' *On Screen* (1972), Ana Mendieta's *Untitled – Glass on body imprints face* (1972), but also works by Pipilotti Rist's *Flatten* (2000) series, producing literary close-ups at the unrecognizable point.

With video art, the screen brought closer the image of an alive artist.[69] So, Rist pushes her face onto the glass recording from the transparent back, simulating flatness of the screen, and the bodily experience of the artist being locked into a monitor, or separated from us by the glass of the monitor. We see recorded space as the reconstructed space of playback in which we are separated by the invisible wall of the medium. The artist is locked inside. Despite the recording glass is small and Rist could not have possibly squeezed herself against the lenses, she simulated a direct contact, over the glass of the playback device, i.e. TV monitor.

Advanced video recording techniques have enforced the question if all visual representations of a person from outside defining self as a corporeal body were not substantial at all. Recordings from the inside of the body with micro cameras, in today's standard procedure of gastroscopy, have redefined self as material beyond-visibility. One of them, Mona Hatoum, in *Corps Étranger* (1994) described a completely different space of the portrait, the inner space of the body, recorded by a swallowed camera. This visually fully unapproachable inside part of us, its bloody and wet environment has also shown the vulnerability of the physical self, as presented to the camera.

One interesting encounter of radically postmodern superimposition of different metrics and systems of interpretation of the personal can be seen in the work of Marta de Menezes titled *Functional Self-Portraits* (2002). The artist fuses imagery of a self-portrait and a portrait with the scan of brain activity, measured with a fMRI scanner.[70] In one particular work from the series, *Self-portrait while Drawing*, the author draws inside the fMRI scanner, and shows the first literary encounter of the self-portrait with the inner content of the face, displaying the beyondness of the banal, surface self, through centuries presented as a mere face, but constantly questioning the inner conditions of the portrayed self.

Before Menezes, Herbert W. Franke's *Digital Einstein* (1973) had already implemented medical diagnostics software in visual arts to render the image of Einstein. While in the artwork by Menezes, a century and a half's quest for inner representation was fulfilled by a basically eugenic method of composite imagery, to which photography as a medium owes its explorations of symbolic systems of interpretation, emancipating it from straight reality.[71] Turning the view of recording self-portraits towards the physical insideness, authors of alternative self-portraiture shifted the definition of the world itself. Inside the body there is no geometry functioning, neither are there subjects

---

69   Michael Rush, *Video Art*, London: Thames and Hudson, 2007.
70   Functional magnetic resonance scanner detects changes in blood flow. Blood flow increases when an area of the brain is used.
71   Picture processing system Bildspeicher N is used in medical diagnostics for evaluation of scintigrams, or radioactive analysis of tissues or other organs, produced by German company Siemens. In Digital Einstein, still, portraits have been processed for the aesthetic purposes. Images produced were offset lithographs taken from computer screen as at the time there were no other direct options of printing possible. Franke photographed the screen in DIA-positives.

and objects, but only a world as it was before, two million years ago as claimed by Vilém Flusser.[72]

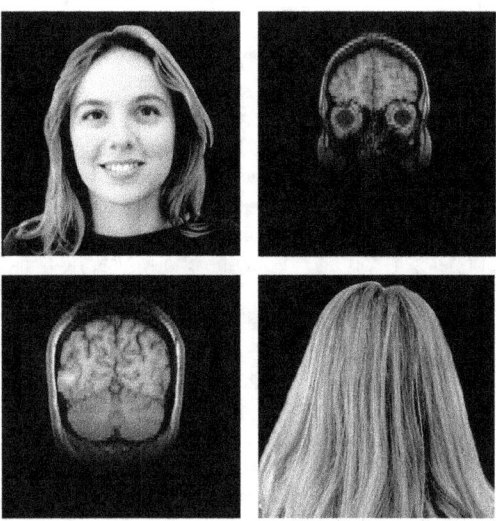

Image 4 – Marta de Menezes: Functional Self-portraits (2002, courtesy of the artist).

Self-capturing, in general, has evolved more dynamically since the invention of photography. Today it is possible to record one's own audio, video, 3D cast, DNA, magnetic field, body temperature, eye diopter, etc. all of which was previously impossible. These different media self-records are in a certain way self-portraits, though they do not always look like the mirror image of the face being based on higher levels of symbolization. As media has shifted to digital recording, it is possible to reduce and subsume different digital signals into one, producing a complex definition of personal measurements, under various systems of metrics.

Media artworks, emphasizing interactivity and participation, have pushed a completely new definition of the self via interactive surfaces, depersonalizing the author. In such artworks, the public is self-portrayed instead of the author, quite unlike the original mirroring of the Narcissus. One of the first interactive pieces produced, in which the artist communicated with the public, is Lynn Hershman Leeson's *Self-portrait as Another Person* (1966-8) consisting of a wax cast of an artist head to which was added an audio tape activated by the audience entering the gallery site. Jeffrey Shaw also communicated the public's self-portrait in his *Self-portrait with the Eiffel Tower* (1988), as well as Alba D'Urbano in *Touch me* (1995). In Shaw's Self-portrait with Eiffel Tower, an image of the public recorded *in situ* is mixed with a by now standardized tourist symbol of Paris, while Alba D'Urbano's public meets the author in an interactive record. In both artworks, the self-reference is portrayed in an active presentation of the audience, rather than the artist. The image appears as not being fixed, but rather time-based, and even more, as interactive.

72   Vilém Flusser, *Into the Universe of Technical Images,* trans. Nancy Ann Roth, intro. Mark Poster, Minneapolis and London: University of Minnesota Press 2011, p. 11.

Media arts, especially participatory and interactive art, have changed the profile of Narcissus once again into the unstable image and unfixed picture. While the unstable image is a result of time-deviation, the unfixed picture is the ephemerality of art media, or to put it simply, both Narcissus and his time-based media change.

Opened for projections of the audience, empathy, and criticism, activist pieces of art introduce a playground for the mirror neurons, rather than play of images. The public is invited to react to the emotional state of the person displaying it, and reactions can range from empathy to disgust. The self-portraitist, furthermore, can communicate via gestures and actions which can range from modest to exaggerated. Today artists deliberately use their bodies to communicate ideas. One of them is an activist artist Šejla Kamerić, who offered her body as an 'empty signifier' to host the idea of Nazism and chauvinism, thus criticizing it.[73] In her work *Bosnian Girl* (2003), she lays out her self-portrait in front of a chauvinist and racist graffiti left behind by an UN soldier in Srebrenica, saying 'No teeth…? A moustache…? Smells like shit…? Bosnian girl!' Speaking simultaneously of the massacre of Muslims from Srebrenica and women from Bosnia and any territory caught in war, this piece has two messages; provocation and pride deriving from empathy, depending on whom the message is sent out to; women, UN forces of the military apparatus. Similarly, Tanja Ostojić's *Looking for a husband with EU passport* (2000-2005) speaks in front of a nation being denied visas because of the war. A woman is trying to escape the local scenario by marrying a foreigner, though under these conditions, as the artwork implies, the marriage connotes human trafficking more than love.

---

73   Similarly, in the serial of artworks named *Self-Portrait as a Part of the Porcelain Export History*, 1999-2001, Ni Haifeng allows his body to be decorated as a porcelain piece, speaking of colonial politics and the image of Chineseness abroad.

II. THE WORLD IN FRONT AND THE WORLD BEHIND OUR BACK

What changed in hundreds of years of self-representation is in the final instance only the mediated space between the author and the audience. This space framing the subject-object relationship, defining completely different ontologies, is conditioned by technology, but also monitored by ideology.

So, to understand selfies, as technologically based and framed self-pictures, it is very important to distinguish between the real, represented, and imaginary space, as residences of objects, subjects and viewers. There are ontological differences among the three spaces. The real space, inhabited by the person self-portraying is represented by the image. The image can show a constructed space, not existing prior to the image perceived by the viewer, for example an architectural plan of a building. Represented space exists even when the viewer turns his head away, and it constructs a place of the viewer, not anyone in particular, but someone with a monocular, unblinking view recognizing real space behind the represented one, to recall James Elkins.[74]

Thus perspective, and perspective-based space is, and Martin Jay recognizes it rightly, atemporal, incorporeal and transcendental.[75] The ideology of such a Cartesian space, based on coordinates and perspectivalism, frames the ideology of ocularcentrism based on a scopic regime, the 'Big Eye' as defined by Jay.[76] So perspective is necessarily a partial and ideological point of view, paradoxically on oneself, connecting to others, describing one's existence in reference to a metric, and thus measurable, relationship of the objects inhabiting the space.

In studies of perspective, to go back to the origin of the discussion, Panofsky's analysis of perspective through Ernst Cassirer's concept of symbolic form, distinguishes the natural [Lat. *perspectiva naturalis*] and artificial [Lat. *perspectiva artificialis*].[77] Artificial perspective was constructed on the stable abstract grounding of its system in Euclidian geometry. Besides space, perspective also defines the Cartesian perception of the self, as objective and neutral.[78] The first, artificial or Euclidian one governs representation of space in Medieval ages and the 16th century, while the second, natural, is a Renaissance ideology of space, that formed around 1400. Panofsky writes;

---

74 James Elkins, *The Poetics of Perspective*, Ithaca and London: Cornell University Press, 1996.
75 Martin Jay, *Downcast Eyes: The Denigration of Vision in Twentieth-century French Thought,* Berkeley: University of California Press, 1994.
76 Jay, *Downcast Eyes.*
77 Erwin Panofsky, *Perspective as Symbolic Form*, trans. Christopher S. Wood, New York: Zone Books, 1991 (1927).
78 Also known as 'Cartesian theatre' – a concept used by Daniel Dennett to described an inner spectacle of self, saying: Cartesian materialism is the view that there is a crucial finish line or boundary somewhere in the brain, marking a place where the order of arrival equals the order of 'presentation' in experience because *what happens there* is what you are conscious of. [...] Many theorists would insist that they have explicitly rejected such an obviously bad idea. But [...] the persuasive imagery of the Cartesian Theater keeps coming back to haunt us—laypeople and scientists alike—even after its ghostly dualism has been denounced and exorcized. Daniel Dennett, *Consciousness explained,* New York City: Back Bay Books, 1992, p. 107.

'Thus the history of perspective may be understood with equal justice as a triumph of the distancing and objectifying sense of the real, and as a triumph of the distance-denying human struggle for control; it is as much a consolidation and systematisation of the external world as an extension of the domain of the self.'[79]

Similarly, Hubert Damisch narrates changes in visual arts from the times when a definition of artificial perspective was first introduced in Pompeii, from Medieval natural perspective to Renaissance artificial space description, and the twisted version of Mannerist concave space, to finally arrive at 'bourgeois artificial perspective'.[80] The final perspective is the one Jay relates to the rise of capitalism.[81] Following the line-up of changes, as I will show, the change has occurred again as another shift, drawing us back to the fish-eyed natural space of the Medieval age in the 'electronic medievalism' characterized by re-awakening of non-Euclidian, irrational, geometries.

Euclidian geometry of antiquity was centered on the visual cone, and had a fixed point of reference, while Renaissance or Albertian geometry, according to Leon Battista Alberti, was organized as a pyramidal structure, defined by the vanishing point, as the point in endless space in which parallel lines seem to meet, to produce a visual, perspectival illusion in conflict with geometry.[82] Alberti has also used a paradigm of the open window [Ita. *finestra aperta*], to define the real word described. Thus, artificial perspective is constructed around three elementary items: line of horizon, reference point which becomes endless in Renaissance, but also the place of the subject that has led to the discovery of the perspectival tool of the photographic camera.[83] This net was, according to Antonio Manetti, for the first time constructed by Filippo Brunelleschi, generally taken as the father of perspective.[84] Brunelleschi's table [Ita. *tavoletta*], described by Manetti in precision, was a painted board with a drawing of the San Giovanni temple, having a hole at the place where a vanishing point was constructed. The viewer had to watch through the hole onto the mirror set on the opposite side, to be able to see the flipped version of the drawing that could have also been made in the mirror.[85] Hubert Damisch names this episode the 'mirror stage of painting,' as it both produces the double of painting and identifies the observer with his/her location in space.[86] The board defines the space that constructs perspective in general, as the distance between mirror and panel that corresponds to the distances in real space, to be able to achieve a total illusion. Moreover, through the hole and the mirror, via spatial constructs, author and observer are connected. The author's view and observer's view perfectly match the point of view that has

---

79   Panofsky, *Perspective as Symbolic Form*, p. 67.
80   Hubert Damisch, *The Origin of Perspective*, trans. John Goodman, Cambridge and London: MIT Press, 1995 (1987).
81   Research in perspective was pushed by the discovery of the endless by Desargues and Kepler, which redefined perspective. Parallel lines, contrary to Euclidian geometries, now will meet in endlessness, defined as the vanishing point. Such projection has reached the full reading with Poncelet's definition of the endless. See: Damisch, *The Origin of Perspective*.
82   Jay, *Downcast Eyes*.
83   More precisely, it is defined by the rule in which all perpendicular lines must meet at 'vanishing point' while all parallels have the same vanishing point on horizon, if the horizon goes through the central vanishing point, according to Panofsky, *Perspective as Symbolic Form*.
84   Jay, *Downcast Eyes*. According to Panofsky, it might have also been Lorenzetti, see: Panofsky, *Perspective as Symbolic Form*.
85   The table reminds both of camera lucida using mirror and camera obscura constructed around a pinhole.
86   Damisch, *The Origin of Perspective*, p. 116.

longer implications in epistemology. Here the 'I' of the author and the observer is defined but also connected, inter-personally, in the Lacanian meaning of the limit of the single point of view on oneself and that I is what Damisch names 'surface being' or a mental projection on the surface.[87] This is also defined as the space previously inhabited by God.[88]

Such a perfectly controlled space is described in Jan van Eyck's portrait of the Arnolfini couple, a late Medieval painting in which two definitions of space collapse. In the painting, space is spread as a proper Euclidian one, its lines are straight and can be drawn directly to a fixed central point, at the same time presenting a completely different space in the mirror positioned at the center of the painting. With this particular painting, art is seen as breaking up with Medieval natural perspective, produced by burning glasses and curved mirrors of the Medieval age, according to Elkins.[89]

The couple that in the first plan of the painting holds hands is orientated frontally to the viewer. The man moves his free, right arm like Christ blessing, holding his pregnant wife with the other one, signaling that he is the one who has 'blessed her'. In front of the couple, their dog lies on the floor. Various objects are spread around, such as; slippers, furniture pieces, characteristic of the bedroom. Symbolic meanings of marriage abound, such as the dog, slippers and a burning candle carrying traditional iconographical meanings of marital faith, home and Holy Spirit.[90]

Besides the event being disputed, one object in painting seems to have occupied an important place.[91] The most central object in this pictorial arrangement is a small round medieval mirror visually posed atop the hands of the couple. This mirror slips the attention of Panofsky, not inspecting the image closely but rather reading into its traditional Catholic iconography, as well as the picture's provenance.[92] And according to it, the mirror iconographically takes the place reserved for pigeons or other symbols of a Holy Ghost.

---

87 Damisch, *The Origin of Perspective*.

88 See for example Berger saying: "The visible world is arranged for the spectator as the universe was once thought to be arranged for God." John Berger, *Ways of Seeing*, London: Penguin books, 1972, p. 16.

89 At the beginning self-portraits included a person in a hierarchical relationship to a ruler. In Egypt, crossing the medieval relationship to the sacred text, artists have been self-portraying in context and in comparison to something of larger importance. The late Medieval self-portrait of Jan van Eyck in the mirror shows a different space description, as it is not one of self-portraits describing the space behind the person observing himself, but rather hiding the self-portrait inside of it, in a proper Medieval manner, still looking the practice of self-maintenance in the mirror as a sign of vanity.

90 Erwin Panofsky, 'Jan Van Eyck's Arnolfini Portrait', *The Burlington Magazine for Connoisseurs* 64.372 (1934): 124.

91 According to Panofsky, the scene is not a simple portrait, but a portrait of the moment of the wedding itself, as it shows different elements of the traditional wedding ceremony, having a presence of ring, hand gesture and witness, who actually is the painter himself. Ibid. There, he opposes the view that the painting actually presents himself who has sealed the marriage in that year, arguing that the painter has married few years before. Panofsky, 'Jan Van Eyck's Arnolfini Portrait'.

92 Under the mirror, in the center of the painting and its most distant point, it is written; 'Johannes de Eyck fuit hic, 1434' meaning not only that the painter is here, but that it is Jan van Eyck himself testifying, leading Panofsky to conclude that the painting itself is a 'pictorial marriage certificate'. Still, as John Searle rightly concluded, the painting must have been painted afterwards as either Eyck was painting the scene or witnessing the ceremony. John R. Searle, '"Las Meninas" and the Paradoxes of Pictorial Representation', *Critical Inquiry* 6.3 (1980): 477-488.

Closely inspected, the mirror shows the perspective of the room reversed. The vanishing point of the whole picture falls into it, returning the image back, as if rewinding a scene, displaying simultaneously a front and back view onto the same stage, or more accurately: providing an integral description. But, the mirror compresses the space laid in front and furthermore, as it is concave, it collapses the perspective, providing a curved interpretation of the space already laid as a straight Euclidian one, with parallel lines that never meet. Compared to the real space laid as first in front of the viewer, in its reflected abstract version in the mirror, the Arnolfini couple find themselves closer to one another. Besides squeezing the farther points of space, the mirror also reduces it, enhancing the view on the distant and not depicting what is positioned in its range.

Such mirrors, concave ones, were indeed the only ones existing and the image mirrored could not have been different in reality. Correlating the visually funded Catholic religion in which God observes and sees everybody and everyone, as well as dominant Cartesian resolution of the Evil Demon into an omnipresent eye of God who guarantees the existence of the world while we are asleep, it is possible to analyze such a mirror in the frame of rather Foucauldian theories of surveillance.[93] Although upgraded technologically to convex and then flat mirrors, concave mirrors are in use even today, as rather simple surveillance tools in shops or at gas stations. Thus, it is a surveillance of the same metaphysical stance that the place of the mirror has visually upgraded, and hangs over the head of the Arnolfini couple. In spite of not showing the Holy Spirit as a white pigeon flying over the hands of the couple, the icono-graphic meaning of this mirror replacement still remains a traditional one. With its distancing ontology, the concave remains the leading visual paradigm of this deeply religious society in which mirrors do not reflect but provide us with an image of an alter-reality above us. It also gives only a partial image, so, at the end of the room a painter appears, while a dog under the legs of a couple disappears from the scene, simultaneously controlling the whole room, as a Big Eye of the original Creator.

93   Michel Foucault, *Discipline and Punish*, Vancouver: Vintage Books, 1995 (1975).

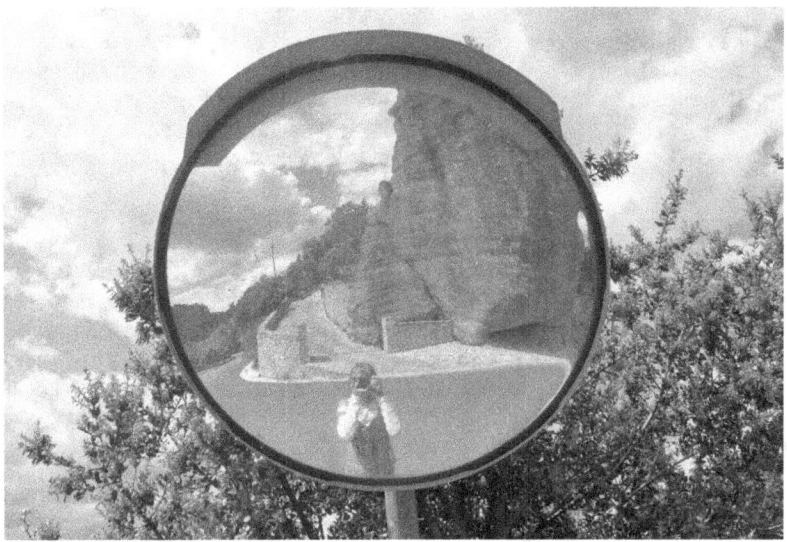

Image 5 – concave mirror view on Meteori in Greece (my photo, 2012).

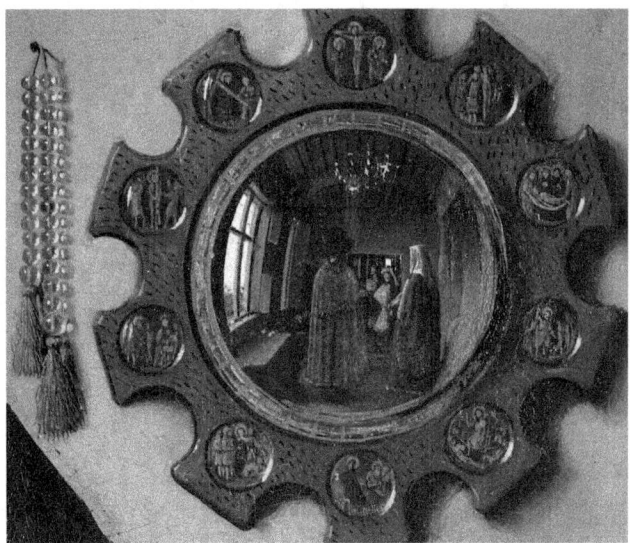

Image 6 – Arnolfini couple, detail (Wikimedia, the work in the public domain).

The reason for the existence of two different world descriptions inside the same picture may be that Van Eyck was experiencing a shift between two spatial ideologies, of Renaissance geometric space fighting an older version of space which was controlling, a concave space that was both metaphysical and physical as the limit of the technology of imaging.[94] So, the mirror in the Arnolfini couple functions both as an eye and a window to the outside world, or in Alberti's definition of perspective – as *finestra aperta*. Contrasting two definitions of space, the ideal Renaissance space and, in this case, unreal non-perspectival space, he was dwelling on ideal space descriptions, which were far more perfect than representations of the couple, more reminiscent of two dolls with large pin heads than humanoids. The clash of Euclidean and non-Euclidian space appears as if speaking of a new metaphysics, the mirror-metaphysics of the world. In such metaphysics, it is indeed a parallel reality that exists, still not mimicking the same qualities as this side of the world.

There are parts of the room which only one space-description provides, as details in, let's name it, Arnolfini's space and details in painter's space. These spaces, according to a curved mirror are divided by a wall and a painter observes the room through the door. But, painter's space conflicts Arnolfini's orthogonal space laid out in front of the painter. Two distinct places and two perspectives appear as twinned ontological realities, so it is not only that viewers see different views of the same scene but face a doubled, matrixed, interpretation of the same room.

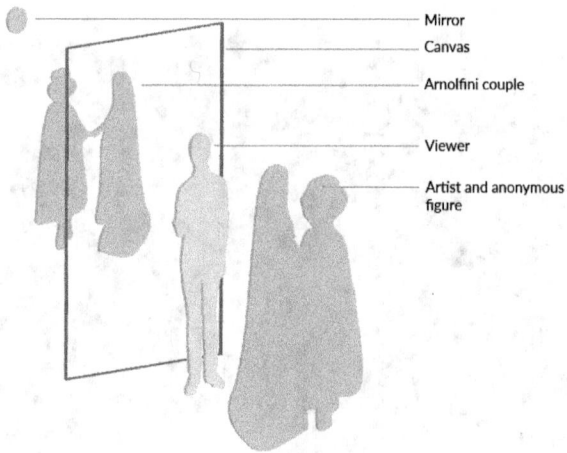

Mirror
Canvas
Arnolfini couple

Viewer

Artist and anonymous figure

Graph 1 – Spacing in Jan Van Eyck's Arnolfini couple. The room in the painting is divided by a wall. Along the artist, a person that is physically not there in the first place is reflected in the mirror. This person may be the viewer who watches the scene. The viewer cannot be behind the artist as he does not see the artist from the back.

---

94   According to Panofsky, his depiction of space was still not geometrically correct. Panofsky, *Jan van Eyck's Arnolfini Portrait.*

Reality Flipped: The Limited Frame of the Mirror

Discovering himself as a viewer, Van Eyck has described viewer's space, in geometry described by the measure between the picture plan and a vanishing point within the picture, also determining the place of the viewer for whom it is constructed.[95] In this painting, the gaze of the viewer flies directly across the first represented space into a second mimicked reality and hits back the viewer, standing at the precise place of a painter, representing the viewer figuratively, as someone in the mirror. Still, it is quite unclear which one of the two figures reflected in the mirror is the viewer, as they are both looking away.[96] We do not know who the figures inside the mirror are, or could be; an older version of the couple, the couple's parents, or the painter and his wife, although keeping with the consistency of perspective and the idea of mirroring it could only be the painter himself.

While in the Arnolfini couple painting viewers are set in Euclidian space, reflected in a non-Euclidian one, which is incorporated inside the first one, in Velázquez' *Las Meninas* (1656) popular for analysis of perspective, viewers are set at the place of the mirror itself. While in Van Eyck the mirrored scene is of lower dimensions, explainable only through the larger set framed by the canvas, in Velázquez' *Las Meninas*, and *Allegory of the Art of Painting*, the explanation for the picture does not reside inside of it, but rather outside, maneuvering viewer's space. Velázquez' painting was discussed by many authors, Foucault being the most prominent one, advocating the thesis that the room in *Las Meninas* has been painted from the point of view of Philippe IV and his wife Mariana of Austria, whose figures are reflected in the mirror behind the back of the artist himself and gazing directly into us.[97]

This painting is full of paradoxes of conflicted spaces.[98] Michel Foucault recognizes two spaces in this picture, the real one and the one reflected in the mirror, being two incompatible visibilities depicted by the act of observing in the mirror.[99] One space is lived, while the other constructed, similarly to Jan van Eyck's picture.[100] Spaces are also distinguished as zones of the visible and invisible. In the first space, without the royal couple, viewers are offered a room

---

95   More accurately; if they are about 45 degrees to the picture plan, the distance among the vanishing point and central vanishing point, according to Panofsky is equal to distance between the viewer's eye and picture plan. Panofsky, *Jan van Eyck's Arnolfini Portrait*.

96   Seems only the husband Arnolfini looks straight onto us, welcoming us, in a way, by his open arm and explanative attitude.

97   Michel Foucault, *The Order of Things*, New York: Pantheon Books, 1970 (1966).

98   In relation to the audience placement and observation of the limited frame of the mirror, what comes to my visual attention at first glance is that the lighting is quite uncommon to Velázquez, and European painting in general. The lighting comes from the right, instead of the left. Light from the left is a characteristic organization for most of paintings of the time; Rembrandt's portraits, Vermeer's depiction, among others. Such light fits the common European way in which the light falls when reading, from left to right, but also with right-handed writing. While there are no other paintings of Velázquez' studio and self-portraits after which it could be clearer if he was left or right handed, there are portraits of Infanta, in which the light falls from left to right, defining the room in which scenes are painted. According to the audience placement, the scene of *Las Meninas* seems to be painted in the mirror itself, so we see a painting flipped. Further the painter stands behind the back of Infanta, so it would be impossible he had painted details he could not see without assistance of a mirror set in front of the scene, as Infanta and the dwarves face.

99   Foucault, *The Order of Things*.

100 Construction and anticipation of place was a topic of analysis of Alpers. See: Svetlana Alpers, 'Interpretation without Representation, or, the Viewing of Las Meninas', *Representations* 1 (1983): 30-42.

with figures and numerous details, while in the second space, faced with traditional portraits they are not being provided any space descriptions. According to Foucault, observers are given the privilege to look from the king's perspective being saluted by most of the protagonists in the picture; the painter, little Infanta, a known court dwarf Maribarbola and another dwarf, dog and the servant gazing from the back.[101] Positioned into a scene directly observed by the King and Queen, we, the observers, too are being observed by them.

Still, this position, bringing us through the eyes of a royal couple that is mediated by the mirror, is reconstructed through the eyes of a painter. But he is the one not seeing himself contrary to Van Eyck who looks at himself. The placing of the painter produces a paradox of space exchange in the picture, analyzed by Foucault, Leo Steinberg and Searle. Foucault has proposed drawing a triangle between the painter's eyes, invisible place occupied by the model and the surface of the canvas in *Las Meninas*, while Steinberg in his interpretation, has defined the triangle between the real, reflected, and depicted, showing the three spaces as representing representation (or the painting process itself).[102] Steinberg claims that the mirrored image is not actually representing the royal couple present at the place of the viewer, but mirrors the image of the painting whose front we do not see.[103] The mirror thus depicts the inverted painting, but also a couple standing in front of us, thus the mirror 'transmits data from two disparate places [...] yet the two are the same.'[104] According to Searle, the picture is inhabited by even more paradoxes, becoming the first painting painted 'from a point of view of the model and not from that of the artist'.[105] Namely, and visible in graphics by Searle; the artist finds himself at the place of the object too, whereas we find ourselves at the place of the artist, and the object. Searle dwells on what happens if we get protagonists back into their original places. He calculates as in a chess play, that if a painter goes back to his original space of an artist, we get a classic self-portrait, but if the King and Queen go back to the place of the object (now the artist), we get a paradoxical loop, in which Velázquez paints the king who then paints Velázquez back.[106] Finally, by removing the mirror from the scene, the paradox is even more enlarged, as in Gustave Courbet's *Painter's Studio* (1854–1855) in which the artist is seen from the back.[107] Searle concludes 'the painter cannot satisfy the condition of this picture.'[108]

---

101 All being identified by Francisco Javier Sánchez Cantòn, in *Las Meninas Y Sus Personajes,* Barcelona: Editorial Juventud, 1943.

102 Analyzing the perspective through the collapse of orthogonal lines, the focal point falls on the person at the door entrance. Analyzing the room itself, more precisely the wall in the back, the central viewpoint falls on the mirror in the back. Furthermore, there are three realities depicted through the view of three man in the painting; painter, person in the back observing the scene and the mirror, and these are real space, as seen by a person in the back, depicted space represented on the canvas of painter and mirrored or reflected space in the mirror, being reality, illusion and replica, as three modalities of the image. Leo Steinberg, 'Velázquez' "Las Meninas"', *October* 19 (1981): 45-54.

103 Steinberg, 'Velázquez' "Las Meninas"'.

104 Steinberg, 'Velázquez' "Las Meninas"', p. 52.

105 John R. Searle, '"Las Meninas" and the Paradoxes of Pictorial Representation', *Critical Inquiry* 6.3 (1980): 483.

106 Searle, '"Las Meninas" and the Paradoxes of Pictorial Representation'.

107 An even more paradoxical positioning is in Vermeer's *Allegory of Painting*, in which he sits himself with his back turned backwards to us. It is the real room in which many of Vermeer's objects were sitting, but here we can see someone else sitting in the room, with his back orientated to us, without looking at himself in the mirror. It is the fictional depiction of the painter in the scene.

108 Searle, '"Las Meninas"' and the Paradoxes of Pictorial Representation', p. 483.

As with all paradoxes, it seems, that even this one can be resolved by set theory, in which the main question posed would be; who is outside of the defined system, or who is the audience? According to audience studies, it is not probable that Velázquez would have ever known that we would hang the picture in a museum, so he has probably just encountered original commissioners as the only public, royal couple sees itself.[109] So, it is the institutionalization of art that produced a paradox, as recognized by Searle.[110]

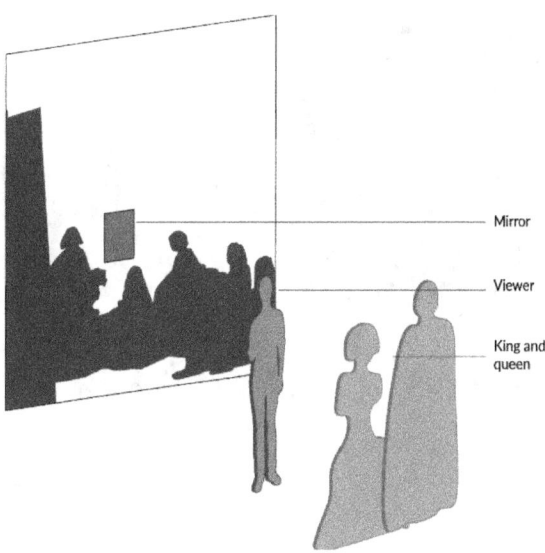

Graph 2 – Spacing in Velasquez' Las Meninas according to Foucault. In the front of the scene the princesses, chaperone and artist are physically present. In the back the mirror shows a reflection of two figures (presumably the Queen and King). When analyzed, it is possible to conclude - the viewer is positioned in the middle.

Convex Mirrors Selfie

With the invention of technologies for the production of new types of mirrors, another reality of descriptions emerged. Convex mirrors defined a completely different universe than the one described by a concave, controlling mirror.

The 'world' presented in convex media appeared as a self-contained universe curved inwards.[111] Parmigianino's self-portrait in a convex mirror is one of these paintings that has shown a complete collapse of the outside world, that could only be described as similar to the physical reaction of implosion, and contrary to expansive explosion. There is indeed some space appearing in this self-portrait, as it also appears in Van Eyck or Vermeer, but this space

---

109 The picture is in the collection of Museo Nacional del Prado.
110 'When an artist using mirrors paints a self-portrait of a familiar and conventional kind, none of the axioms of classical representation are violated.' Searle, '"Las Meninas" and the Paradoxes of Pictorial Representation', p. 484.
111 So, it is possible, as visible in Pontormo's painting of the Duke Alessandro de' Medici, who looks at us while drawing a self-portrait, still drawing a female figure, is seeing us as the mirror.

has hardly any recognizable form. It has the shape of a claustrophobic bowl and one can feel as a small golden fish in aquarium. This room, namely, appears smaller than the frame of the picture and moreover the same room and picture meet at the same plan.

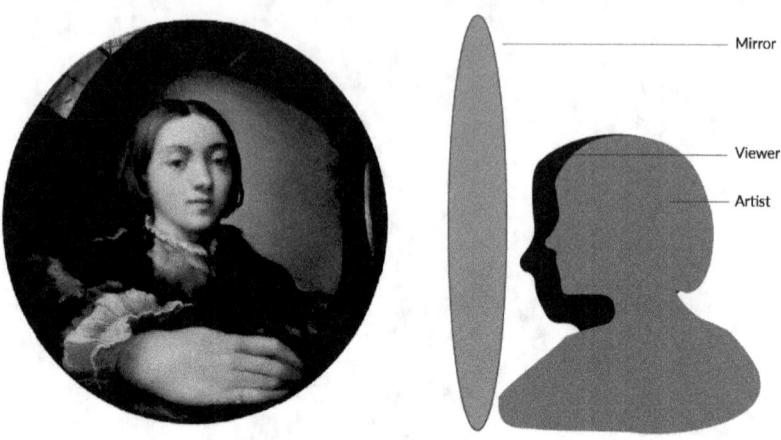

Graph 3 – Spacing in Parmigianino's Self-portrait in convex mirror. Here the space of the artist and viewer almost overlap.

Even in such a compressed zone, where two realities of the straight and curved space, or the surface of painting and a mirror converge, there is a minor space for the viewer. Fusing two distinct realities, of micro and macro-cosmos, Parmigianino has opened a space for contemporary skepticism. Namely, this portrait, screening the mirror rather than the scene mirroring, does not display any reality besides the face of the painter, which we confront behind our back in the mirror, and even more – it leaves no space for the viewer at all. Steinberg thus concludes rightly that via the action of mirroring; it is almost that *we* are becoming Parmigianino.[112] As in Parmigianino's self-portrait, defining the boundaries of the curved space inside the frame of the picture, a world that is a large bowl squeezed into the picture, selfies produced with a selfie stick squeeze the viewer inside.[113]

The curved space-time was already visible in astronauts' self-portraits in space that had become a genre in itself, already in the 60s, when the astronaut Buzz Aldrin recorded his EVA space photo in 1966. This self-portrait displays Aldrin in a counter-light, with an illuminated planet behind his back. Recent self-portrait of the astronaut Akihiko Hoshide, named the 'ultimate selfie' by Nicholas Mirzoeff, shows an astronaut recorded in front of the sun, floating freely in space while the space-ship he faces is reflected in his helmet, completely covering his face.[114] There, in the reflection of his helmet, the space ship looks like a small toy, in front of which even the sun is overly small. The real space of the astronaut has changed, being the

112 Steinberg, 'Velázquez' "Las Meninas"'.
113 And here the image and the picture do not match at all.
114 Nicolas Mirzoeff, *How to see the World*, London: Penguin Books, 2015.

screen of the computer, the space ship in front, producing a second plan as secondary reality itself. The outer reality is described as disproportional and ephemeral, almost as abandoned behind. The astronaut's privileges of seeing the outer form of a curved space are changing also the relationship of the selves to the external reality, as if changing the size of the river in which Narcissus self-reflects.

Jumping a bit further in time, to the invention of photographic media, the dominant style in arts profoundly changed, according to many contemporary authors, as for example Jonathan Crary.[115] Photography as a technical medium, has stayed closely related to Cartesian coordinates of space in arts, which itself is based in Euclidian geometry.[116] This close connection to classic geometry was emphasized by many authors, Flusser among others sees photography as even more Cartesian than Descartes himself;

'Apparatuses, meanwhile, these simulations of Cartesian thought, have succeeded. They are omniscient and omnipotent in their universes. For in these universes, a concept, an element of the program of the apparatus, is actually assigned to every point, every element of the universe.'[117] Importance of defining photography as a perspectival tool is important for understanding what Elkins names schizophrenic definition of perspective, the split between geometry and optics, mathematical and physiological space.[118]

Perspectival technologies change cultures, Edward Shanken has noted.[119] Perspective organizes the placement of the viewer, and differences occur with media. In painting, viewer's space is fixed but adaptable. The placement is arranged by perspectival calculus relative to the height at which the painting is hanged. With newer media, such as photography, the viewer's space may be directed, but is not found at a single spot. Namely, it replicates and multiplies, as does the experience of the original viewer, who goes through the same space, though does not necessarily have the same experience, seeing the same photograph reproduced for example in different advertisements. Thus, perspective in photography is defined as an ontological tool.[120] When this media is interactive, the viewer's space is being exchanged, or even offered as directly mirrored. Namely, it is not only that with space descriptions we are learning space, but while viewing we are also changing and constructing it, completely.

115 Jonathan Crary, *Techniques of the Observer: On Vision and Modernity in the Nineteenth Century*, Cambridge and London: MIT Press, 1992.
116 Crary, *Techniques of the Observer*.
117 Vilem Flusser, *Towards Philosophy of Photography*, London: Reaktion Books, 2006, p. 68.
118 Elkins claims perspective divides the viewer from the viewed. Elkins, *The Poetics of Perspective*.
119 Edward Shanken, *Virtual perspective and the artistic vision. A genealogy of Technology, Perception and Power*, Rotterdam: ISEA, 1996.
120 The change between monocular and binocular vision is, according to Hershenson, in the angle of view; monocular being limited to 120 degrees, while binocular being expanded for about 40 on each side. So, total binocular vision turns 200 degrees in total. Maurice Hershenson, *Visual Space Perception*, Cambridge and London: Bradford Book, MIT Press, 1999.

Proxemic Distance

While Renaissance, as announced in Jan van Eyck, introduced a subject-defined space, the same space collapsed with Mannerism, in Parmigianino's self-portrait. Subject-space will be squeezed even further with self-portraits based on lens technology, now allowing a voyeuristic insight into the scene, announced by the arm of Parmigianino's self-portrait. Parmigianino's arm, visible in the painting, emerges from his body and enters the viewer's personal space, crossing the subject's or Parmigianino's reality onto our space as if he tries to test if we our-selves are real by touching us. Simultaneously, the personal space of Parmigianino is literally caught and framed in between his arm and his body.

This long tradition that started with Parmigianino, in which we actually see the arm of the author inside the frame, is fully exemplified in self-portraits in which the arm is the only part of the self-representation, simultaneously closing us, the viewers, in the intimate body space of the author.[121] This arm, that points back to the author of the material picture creator, is accord-ing to Paul Frosch 'deictically indexical, inclusively com-posed, reflexive and reflex – alters and deepens the relationship between photographic mediation and the impulse to sociability.'[122] That deictic arm shows that there is no one else in the place of the photographer, bridging the physical distance once reserved for two people in communication, thus – indicating the absence of the inter-mediator too.

Such symbolic empty space, in which a subject is communicating with a missing photogra-pher, is also visible in the iconic image of Josef Koudelka displaying the time on his clock, with his arm stretched inside the frame. The arm closes the space in front of him and us, the way we watch with him through his eyes. We, the audience, are participating in the empty streets of Prague, experiencing its strange quietness minutes before the Prague uprising in 1968. A similar position, but with a different effect, is taken in a series of photographs by Arno Rafael Minkkinen. His arm enters the viewing space of the photograph, producing a strange angle and positions in the landscape set in front. Occasionally it produces paradoxes of sizes, so his arm seems as the arm of a giant, changing the landscape, still having no political but rather aesthetical message, but also an ancient body measure of space.

Contrary to Koudelka and Minkkinen, whose arms are real and deictic, there is on the market an artificial arm functioning as a selfie stick. Instead of a piece of metal, the author of a selfie holds a realistic cast of an arm that anticipates the viewer, symbolically dragging him inside the scene. The selfie produced is trans-personal, as the hand does not define a viewer more accurately, but there are constantly new visitors who are dragged into the scene. No more laying out a personal space, of the photographer, but a space of the person other than the author, present as an object put in the front, the arm suggests a mystic presence behind the picture, an invisible companion in whose place viewers find themselves, becoming at the same time photographers.

---

121   Jill Walker-Rettberg, *Seeing Ourselves through Technology,* London: Palgrave Macmillan, 2014, p. 9.
122   Paul Frosh, 'The Gestural Image: The Selfie, Photography Theory and Kinesthetic Sociability',
      International Journal of Communication 9 (2015): 1623.

Spectator

With changes of space, now being filled with iconographic objects, the position of the viewer changes too. Foucault has recognized this gaze:

> We, the spectators, are an additional factor. Though greeted by that gaze, we are also dismissed by it, replaced by that which was always there before we were: the model itself. But, inversely, the painter's gaze, addressed to the void confronting him outside the picture, accepts as many models as there are spectators; in this precise but neutral place, the observer and the observed take part in a ceaseless exchange.[123]

This hypothetical, anticipated gaze of the viewer, laid out in many classic paintings, conditioned positions of the real viewers and dominant interpretations of the pieces.

Self-portraits communicate with viewers by the use of mirrors or mirror-based technology. For example, Jan van Eyck places the mirror at the back of Arnolfini couple, which shows the room in which the painter appears in our place. We, the audience in this image, are the painter, not the medium. Contrary to Jan van Eyck, a later and much discussed painting by Velázquez, *Las Meninas* positions the mirror at a similar place to suggest and show the appearance of the King and Queen in our place. Although by the position of a mirror suggesting we, the viewers, are a royal couple, this painting was actually made only for their eyes, so the viewer-object relationship carries through an exclusive narrowing.

Contrary to these classic art pieces, media artworks that mobilize participatory action have replaced the place of the original author, by interchanging places of the self-portrait with the portrait of the audience. Selfies go even further, in displacing the viewer, being divided by the screen of the monitor, the medium itself, but also pushing reality behind one's back. Mobile phone culture, in which everyone is an artist, and media art, in which the audience participates in art, both close the space similarly as in times of medieval ages, before the invention of geometric perspective, by imprisoning us within the media loop, and denying our own position as separate agents in the process of communication. As tools become smaller, the space for representing others, even non-present audience also miniaturizes, and the subject withdraws inside a small universe, as small as a tiny birdcage.

---

123 Michel Foucault, *The Order of Things*, New York: Pantheon Books, 1970 (1966), p. 5.

III. NARCISSUS AND HIS EVIL TWIN

He who sees himself in the mirror,
sees himself well
He who sees himself well,
Knows himself well
He who knows himself well
Takes little ride in himself.[124]

Narcissus and Echo

The myth of Narcissus is commonly invoked in the interpretation of selfies, but also self-portraits.[125] The myth, originally developed by Romans and narrated in Ovid's *Metamorphoses*, is an apotheosis of sterility, based on the real infertility of a flower narcissus, having no seeds for its procreation.[126] Narcissus, son of the water nymph Linope, is punished by Goddess Nemesis for ignoring the love of the nymph Echo. He is condemned to become like a flower which name he wears and stare into his own reflection with which he will fatally fall in love, thus ending his life. Merging picture and image leads to a fatal end, as recognized by Flusser; 'The interaction between the image and person is marked by entropy tending toward death.'[127]

The only witness to this disappearance is a passive Echo, who follows him to his end. The tragic love story, pregnant with egoism; the ego-centrism of Narcissus and submissiveness of Echo; sadism and masochism in which sadism at the end self-destroys, speaks also to the need for communication and the culture of interaction, both of which Narcissus lacks and is incapable of.

While Narcissus is centered on the visual medium, Echo is a sound-based character, producing constant time-delayed sound reverberations, mixed with the voice that he hears in his head. Thus, Narcissus multiplies visually and auditorily. Audio hallucinations create a complete acoustic isolation, schizophrenic illusions of companionship produced in loneliness and solitude, as symptoms of his mad self-love. They form an extended experiential reality, which had not played a larger impact on the scopophilic Western culture.[128]

---

124 Pierre Gringore via Sabine Melchior-Bonnet, *The Mirror: A history*, trans. Katherine H. Jewett, London and New York: Routledge, Taylor and Francis, 2006, p. 136.
125 Already Leon Battista Alberti in *De Pictura* (1435) inaugurated Narcissus as the model for arts by saying; 'Consequently, I used to tell my friends that the inventor of painting, according to the poets, was Narcissus.' Alberti, De Pictura: http://www.noteaccess.com/Texts/Alberti/.
126 Ovid, 8 AD. Hall writes the myth reflects the ancient Greeks' fears that 'a reflection in water could be dragged down or swallowed up, having you soulless, and so doomed to die.' Hall, *The Selfportrait*.
127 Vilem Flusser, *Into the Universe of Technical Images*, trans. Nancy Ann Roth, Minneapolis and London: University of Minnesota Press, 2011, p. 59.
128 I also thank my students of MA Media Art Histories in Krems, 2015/16, for pointing at the importance of auditory effects.

The Extension of Narcissus

But, the question is – has he ever recognized himself in the image? Different theorists approached the myth from various angles. According to some, Narcissus does not know himself but only maintains his own image, while according to others he withdraws from society to contemplate. Foucault recognizes Narcissus as falling into a care of the self, while being totally incapable of arriving at knowledge of the self.[129] Indeed, not recognizing himself, Narcissus is depersonalizing, as would contemporary theory of psychological disorders define.[130]

Marshall McLuhan gave a more contemporary, media related version of the myth.[131] Instead of transmission, his Narcissus has exiled via less tragic mediation:

> The youth Narcissus mistook his own reflection in the water for another person. This extension of himself by mirror numbed his perceptions until he become the servo-mechanism of his own extended or repeated image. The nymph Echo used to win his love with fragments of his own speech, but in vain. He was numb. He had adopted his extension himself and had become a closed system.[132]

According to McLuhan, Narcissus is not aware of himself as a picture, as he does not recognize himself in his self-image. He does not distinguish reality from fiction, as he abstracts himself out of it. The tragedy of this love intensifies as he falls into the illusion that he actually is someone else. His perceptual dissociation from his own body, unaware of sliding towards the water and touching its liquid reflection screen, as if approaching someone else, is a tragedy of pure alienation.

Here McLuhan charmingly explains Narcissus' destiny via a theory of numbing body parts that were, or were to be, amputated and replaced by its technological extension or prosthesis, etymologically connecting Narcissus' name to Greek *arkō* [Gr. narcosis, to-make-numb]. Narcissus exiles his own image, previously modified by the technology of reflection, as he himself is exiled by the technologies he uses. To survive this transition, Narcissus has to auto-amputate his own body parts, his central nervous system. As McLuhan warns, 'Technology (or his variously extended body)'... 'is perpetually modified by it and in turn finds ever new ways of modifying technology', by developing it.[133]

But, according to McLuhan, if Narcissus recognized himself in his image, the result would not be so fatal.[134] If Narcissus knew that he was sinking into his own image, that would be a suicide but disappearing into the image believing it to be someone else is rather a murder. Indeed, the curse says he is punished under the condition; if he does not know himself [Lat.

---

129 Still, as we may read from Foucault's essay, it seems only with the times of Christianity that this approach would appear as immoral, as judged from the society that recognizes itself not as itself, but as a metaphysical 'I' that emanates each individual separately, but the same way.
130 In the depersonalization disorder, a person looking at himself does not see himself, but sees someone else.
131 Marshall McLuhan, *Understanding Media: The Extensions of Man*, Intro. Lewis H. Lapham, Cambridge: MIT Press, 1994.
132 McLuhan, *Understanding Media*, p. 41.
133 McLuhan, *Understanding Media*, p 46.
134 McLuhan, *Understanding Media*.

si se non nouerit], that condition can easily be extended to; if his passion is not rationalized, or if he is not using his introspection but rather *extraspection* as a cognitive model.[135]

Space of Narcissus

Analyzing the painting of Caravaggio, Mieke Bal goes even further in proving that Narcissus is not aware of the medium.[136] In the painting, Narcissus visibly falls in love with an 'image without a body', or more accurately – a fiction, as indeed, Ovid writes, 'he loves an insubstantial hope and trusts in a substance which is only a shadow' [Lat. *spem sine corpore amat, corpus putat esse, quod umbra est*].[137]

Caravaggio's Narcissus in Bal's interpretation is pushing his knee to defend the space of his self-loving activity. His knee is hostile to the viewer, breaking up the surface of the painting, brutally entering into the viewer's space. More metaphorically, it directly kicks the viewers' eye. The knee crosses the barrier of the surface of the painting to enter our space, at the height of the observer's eye, blocking our gaze so he, and he alone, can enjoy his own company. With his aggressive knee, he shows he does not need us in his self-adoration. He also does not need the Caravaggio picture at all, all he needs is his own lovely image. And it is rather we who need Narcissus' picture as a cautionary tale about tainted self-love.

Behind the two surfaces, are the twofold actions of Narcissus, loving and defending at the same time, indicating he is aware of us, as he is not willing to expose himself to our voyeuristic sight. Nevertheless, we see and indeed watch someone who does not want us to watch him at all. We are the voyeurs, the ones who are transgressing, present in the constructed space of the image trying to cross the physical barrier of the picture, by that hostile act.

Simultaneously to the act of expelling the viewer, Narcissus performs yet another action, totally inverted gentle act of self-loving of that self-picture he simultaneously does not recognize as self-image. This erotic, or more consistently; homo-erotic affair he has with 'other' self, although describes a pure solipsist universe, cannot be seen as a perfect one, as Narcissus is not aware he is actually alone.

Narcissus' picture of the world, projected on the water, is completely different from ours, seen on the painted screen. Finding ourselves staring at the knee, we are in the position of the lonely Echo, the faithful lover committing herself to become a shadow, an alter ego and a reporter, a spy, and only witness to his existence. What we, as viewers see in Caravaggio's

---

135 Still, maybe more interesting would be to rephrase it for the case of visual culture into; he is involved TO image, no INTO the image.

136 Mieke Bal, *Looking in: The Art of Viewing*, London: Routledge, Taylor and Francis, 2004, p. 241.

137 This, quite erotic, as Freud noted, falling in love is described in the following verses:
'Oh I am he! Oh, now I know for sure
The image is my own; its for myself
I burn with love; I fan the flames I feel
What now? Woo or be wooed? Why woo at all?
Would I might leave my body! I could wish
(Strange lover's wish!) My love were not so near'
Ovid via Simon Blackburn, *Mirror, Mirror: The Uses and Abuses of Self Love*, Princeton and Oxford: Princeton University Press, 2014, p. 38.

painting is Echo's report, a story of her own pain. Still, Narcissus sees neither Echo nor us, as he is self-preoccupied. Division among Echo's and Narcissus's universe is both physical and meta-physical, staring while gazing at the same thing, both looking at it as an object of desire. What Echo wants is different from his unmediated and physical body, while what he wants merely is his mediated illusion.

Besides the double action, of expelling others and loving oneself, there is yet another doubling in the image. There are two surfaces in this image: water and painting. Two separate media of reflection described in the painting are the painting itself and the water, both provide a different type of reflection, so we do not see what Narcissus does. One media produces images, the other pictures. In other representations of the self too there are barriers that sometimes function as screens for self-projections. There are 'this' and 'that' worlds, viewer's space of existence and the simulated space that the viewer sees. Still, the capacity of the viewer to be out of the limited two-dimensional world and literally 'have' another dimension of viewing, paints the scene as a tragedy of the solipsistic universe itself, based on a psychological withdrawal claiming that the one that is not with us should be necessarily unhappy. But, as John Durham Peters nicely formulated, Narcissus did not need to overcome death.[138]

Exile Into Someone Else

There is little connection between the original Narcissus and the self-portrait, or even Caravaggio's portrait of him. Self-portraiture stabilizes the image of narcissistic self-mirroring that the original Narcissus does not need at all. Namely, Narcissus mediates into the image that is a mere reflection that is constantly changing. After mediation, he is no longer himself – as he never is himself – but he is constantly someone else. Still, he is hedonistically aware of his exile into a new body, based on self-reflection, inhabiting a different, virtual territory, feeling the mediation as a continuous process. The technology of the contemporary age allows us to do what Narcissus did not need at all – simultaneous recording and viewing, capturing a full narcissistic ecstasy.

Self-portrait is rather a picture, an object that can transfer, time-wise and space-wise, forwarding the image to the future, disconnecting it from the original medium of self-reflection into the water. And indeed, why should Narcissus need to detach from the original picture and save it for the future if there is none beside him in his solipsistic universe? Peters quotes Heidegger:

"Soliloquy is the product and reflex of converse with others; social communication not an effect of soliloquy." Thus solipsism would be the luxury of already socialized individuals who had forgotten their histories.[139]

Still, the ultimate solipsist does not need a picture, but it is rather the one suspicious of his own identity. A solipsist is convinced that none – apart from himself – exists, concluding that he is living in an utterly private universe. A relativist, to the contrary, claims that his personal identity has profoundly changed since the last moment. Both practices have in common a

---

138 Peters defines a distinction between transmission and recording, as overcoming distance and death. John Durham Peters, *Speaking Into the Air: A History of the Idea of Communication,* Chicago: University of Chicago Press, 1999, p. 143.
139 John Dewey, *Experience and Nature*, Carbondale: Southern Illinois University Press, 1988, pp. 135, 136 via Peters, *Speaking into the Air*, p. 18.

skeptical tradition, still, while solipsism is an unsolvable position being a consequence of methodological doubt, skepticism of personal identity is rather a sophistic challenge, well-illustrated by Epicharmus, who mocks his creditor claiming he is not the same person he was at the time of signing the contract, so he cannot then possibly be taken to be in responsible for it.[140] Epicharmus' claims are even more radicalized in Cratylus claim that 'you cannot step into the "same" river even once'.[141] Whereas solipsism withdraws the person into his own territory, skepticism of personal identity states that even a subject is unstable and cannot be caught and captured, which is clear in the motif of photography. Still, Solipsism and Skepticism are connected in terms that a failure to recognize the world while not being seen pushes one to the recording of it, as Leonardo once noted, comparing a painter to a mirror: 'which copies everything placed in front of it without knowledge of the same'.[142] Similarly, a narcissist falls into small deaths between two self-perceptions.

Contrary to Narcissus, Dorian Gray has managed to finally exteriorize, or fully mediate, into the picture.[143] In the case of Dorian Gray, the paradox of representability is produced by the split between self-representation and self-imaging. There is a picture, as a carrier, and the ideal image, as an imagined model and they do not resemble each other.

Nevertheless, in both cases of self-representation, the person self-deteriorates, exiling into another visual stance. Dorian moves into the picture and contrary to Narcissus, who dies into the image, he does not decay, but the image does instead of him.[144] The ultimate goal is not a death of painting, but the destruction of self-projection. To be more precise; while Narcissus exiles in the image, Gray's image of youth exiles into him, exchanging places with his decaying body, so that he is becoming a picture. In other words, he materializes himself into the picture, as most of the artists, leaving only a grandiose self-image not matching any present reality, while Narcissus abstracts himself, leaving his own body behind. Gray, thus, is the 'dark version' of Narcissus, his actual inversion. He is the original narcissist, while Narcissus is not – as he is not himself.

Psychology of Narcissus

According to Sigmund Freud, Erich Fromm and the most recently Christopher Lasch, there are two types of narcissism; primary and secondary. The concept of primary narcissism refers to an ordinary libidinal investment in the self, which is a precondition of erotic love, according to Freud, who distinguishes two phases, infantile and anxious, first being characterized by emptiness and discontent, while the second by egomaniac and aggressive narcissism.[145] This

---

140 Raymond Martin and John Barresi, *The Rise and Fall of Soul and Self. An Intellectual History of Personal Identity*, Ithaca and London: Columbia University Press, 2010.
141 Martin and Barresi, *The Rise and Fall of Soul and Self*, p. 12.
142 Leonardo da Vinci, *Notebooks*, Oxford: Oxford University Press, 2008: 212.
143 Story by Oscar Wilde (1890), movie: *The Picture of Dorian Gray* (dir. Albert Lewin, 1945).
144 Starting with invocation;
      'I sent my Soul through the Invisible,
      Some letter of that After-life to spell:
      And by and by my Soul return'd to me,
      And answer'd "I Myself am Heav'n and Hell."'
      Omar Khayyam, *The Rubaiyat*, 1120 A.C.E, available at: http://classics.mit.edu/Khayyam/rubaiyat.html.
145 Freud, *On Narcissism*. Note here, also McLuhan has called this age the one of Anxiety.

is a difference, according to Freud, in the way *libido* and *destrudo* of a newborn narcissist, sometimes also called 'biological narcissism' and adult narcissist work.[146] A primary, newborn narcissist does not distinguish between the outer and inner world, while a secondary narcissist, an adult, builds up all the meanings in regard to himself. Erich Fromm similarly distinguishes between two stages of narcissism.[147] Contrary to primary narcissism, which is a survival tool, secondary narcissism, according to Fromm, is pathological, centered on self-grandiosity, phantasm of omnipotence, easily turned into an aggressive behavior.[148]

With reference to both Freud and Fromm, Lasch concentrated on contemporary, pathological Narcissus, who has a phantasm of omnipotence that includes a right to exploit others as well as a need for the gratification.[149] He also distinguished between two types of narcissism; narcissism as the libidinal instrument of the self, serving as a precondition for love, and narcissism as the incorporation of grandiosity, he names secondary or pathological narcissism.[150] What a secondary narcissist experiences as a consequence of delusion according to Lasch, is an inner emptiness, repressed rage, pseudo self-insight, intense fear of getting old and ugly, fear of competition, decline of a play spirit, among other symptoms, commonly manifested through calculating seductiveness and nervous self-deprecatory humour.[151] Those indicating signs of secondary narcissism will end up in a master middle life crisis at the moment they realize they are getting old and they have invested their lives in managing people not goods. For that, according to Lash, Narcissus is usually socially condemned, being perceived as anti-social, for his vanity, self-admiration, and self-glorification.[152]

Online Narcissuses

As diagnosed by Lasch, narcissism has become a cultural phenomenon.[153] Our contemporary post-digital age has its own variants. According to researchers Laura Buffardi and Keith Campbell, online narcissism is often characterized by a large number of friends, developing a sub-symptom of 'grandiose exhibitionism'.[154] Inflation consists of seeking a larger and larger audience.[155] Paradoxically enough, this pluralisation does not make one unique. Online life provides an opportunity to the user to present a real self and a possible self, as well as to share named and anonymously, directly and indirectly.[156] Besides inventing oneself or one's own image, a person may exaggerate or completely reinvent himself, embodying the idea of the new self, as the Other, so Hayles notes:

---

146 McLuhan, *Understanding Media*.
147 Erich Fromm, *The heart of man*, New York: Lantern Books, 2010 (1964).
148 Secondary narcissism appears as the complete opposite to a strong self-love.
149 Some other theories distinguish between: Authority Narcissist, Self-Admiring Narcissist, Superiority Narcissist, and Exploitative Narcissist.
150 Lasch, *The Culture of Narcissism*.
151 McLuhan, *Understanding Media*.
152 Lasch, *The Culture of Narcissism*.
153 Ibid.
154 Laura E. Buffardi and W. Keith Campbell, 'Narcissism and Social Networking Web Sites', *Personality and Social Psychology Bulletin*, 34.10 (2008): 1303-1314.
155 Christopher J. Carpenter, 'Narcissism on Facebook: Self-promotional and Anti-Social Behavior', *Personality and Individual Differences*, 52.4 (2012): 482-486.
156 Soraya Mehdizadeh, 'Self-Presentation 2.0: Narcissism and Self-Esteem on Facebook' *Cyberpsychology, Behavior, and Social Networking*, 13.4 (2010): 357-364, DOI: 10.1089/cyber.2009.0257.

The overlay between the enacted and the represented bodies is [...] a contingent production, mediated by a technology that has become so entwined with the production
of identity that it can no longer meaningfully be separated from the human subject.[157]

Because of ties to the identity of this exaggerated, unreal person, it speaks more of itself than
an ordinary representation in a self-portrait ever would. It uncovers the hidden, subconscious
drives, wishes, feelings, and ideas that would otherwise stay hidden behind the neutral
appearance of the object.

Consequently, a self that is neither narrated through specific moments of life, nor constructed
in a systematic interpretation, becomes a mere bodily experience of one's temporary existence.
There is no nostalgia for past events in photo albums, nor is there a utopia of the future when
the ideal self will be achieved. Only a body that pulsates in time-place coordinates always
only exists in the moment 'now'.

The Other of Echo

Narcissism, as defined by Lasch, provides a ground for interpretation of the self-picture based
culture both as incapable of distinguishing the Self and the Other, but also in the secondary
phase of manipulating them. Narcissus, on the other hand, is the one neglecting the Other
or Echo, who does not need a picture at all. Neither the narcissist nor Narcissus objectifies
and knows himself, or his self-image, and neither is able to self-report accurately in a picture.

Taking into account the history of self-portraiture, the relationship to the Other via images can
be defined in three distinct relationships; knowing oneself as the Other, mirroring or identifying
with the Other, and self-inventing oneself as the Other. I will name these relationships as; the
relationship of subject to the objectified self, the inner psychotherapeutic relationship with
oneself, as a cure for oneself, and a pathological cultural phenomenon of narcissism, being
also the ideology of the Self.

The first psychological relation of knowing the self as the Other is based on the externalization
of the self. 'Externalization and objectification of self' as Gen Doy noted, by which the subject
has to become an object and be perceived as such by itself, is also tautological.[158] Seeing
oneself as the object in terms of classic media was literary possible only if a wandering soul
could have left its body of residence, and, at least for a moment, dwell on an out-of-body-ex-
perience; such as in hallucinating experiences with drugs, lucid dreaming, temporary death,
an after-death divination, or by residing in some other body – what Maurice Merleau-Ponty
named 'primordial ontology of vision' prior to subjects and objects.[159] With new digital tools,
such metempsychosis become partially possible, in effects as mediated mirroring, or by dupli-
cation of the body, by which it is the sensorial experience that is separated from the presence.

---

157   Katherine N. Hayles, *How We Became Posthuman: Virtual Bodies in Cybernetics, Literature, and
      Informatics*, Chicago: University of Chicago Press, 1999, p. XIII.
158   Gen Doy, *Picturing the Self: Changing View on the Subject in Visual Culture*, London: I.B.Tauris, 2005,
      p. 36.
159   Maurice Merleau-Ponty, *The Visible and the Invisible*, trans. Alphonso Lingis, Evanston: Northwestern
      University Press, 1968, https://monoskop.org/images/8/80/Merleau_Ponty_Maurice_The_Visible_and_
      the_Invisible_1968.pdf defines images without referent and images prior to referent.

This process of self-objectification is threefold. According to Doy it contains; subjectivity of the process, impossibility of representing subjectivity, and subjectivity of viewing the self.[160] These three layers can also be elaborated at the level of motifs. Crozier and Greenhalgh already mentioned the subjectivity of the process, noting the importance of interpreting motifs behind recording a portrait, which in the arts can be different.[161] The second criteria would be a selection made upon the settlement and recording process as well as the choice among photographs that have succeeded in narrating the ideal picture of the self. The third one would be related to the public, analyzing the gaze.

Following previously elaborated theory of types of representations via self-portraits, selfies can be analyzed. The reasons of self-recording are orientated to self-managing in terms of different self-descriptions; the self as being a prominent member of a social group or establishment, the self as a role, the self as a state and condition, and the self as a body, each being introduced at certain part of history and continued as a form till nowadays. But interpretations get complicated once a personal identity of the creator is not known so we can easily misinterpret the original motive or drive. Amelia Jones warns that with each process of objectification there is a subsequent change in the subject, saying; technologies 'render and/ or confirm the self, paradoxically objectifying the self so to prove its existence as a subject'.[162] By correlating technology of recording a personal self-portrait to the relationship to oneself, as direct self-knowing, indirect self-mirroring, or avoidable and superficial self-inventing, it is possible to grasp more meanings of contemporary culture hidden behind any distributed image of the self, in terms of the technology of self-representation. And that is from where the need to self-record arrives, in the need to stabilize the meaning of the self.

---

160   Doy, *Picturing the Self*, p. 36.
161   W. Ray Crozier and Paul Greenhalgh, 'Self-Portraits as Presentations of Self', *Leonardo* 21.1 (1988):
       29-33.
162   Amelia Jones, *Self/Image, Subject, Technology, Representation and the Contemporary Subject*, London
       and New York: Routledge, Taylor and Francis, 2006, p. XVII.

IV. FROM ECHO'S POINT OF VIEW

"But I never looked like that!" – How do you know? What is the "you" you might or might not look like? Where do you find it – by which morphological or expressive calibration? Where is your authentic body? You are the only one who can never see yourself except as an image: you never see your eyes unless they are dulled by the gaze that rests upon the mirror or the lens (I am interested in seeing my eyes only when they look at you): even and especially for your own body, you are condemned to the repertoire of its images.[163]

Other in the Mirror

The most demanding thing for Narcissus, who runs away from himself, is knowing the self. Sabine Melchior-Bonnet notes:

To see oneself in the mirror, to identify oneself, requires a mental operation by which the subject is capable of objectivising himself, of separating what is outside from what is inside. This operation can be successful if the subject recognizes the reflection as his own likeness and say, "I am the other of that other".[164]

And in this conclusion, it is Narcissus who fails, not recognizing the image as other, neither recognizing himself in that other.[165]

Contrary to McLuhan, who thought Narcissus exiles his own body into the image, abandoning his own body numbed, Julia Kristeva analyzed how he withdraws into the most secure place, in his self-sufficient heaven.[166] Kristeva states the sign of narcissistic crisis is rather the abjection caused by contradictory causes; too much of strictness on the part of the Other or lapse of the Other.[167] This withdrawal is not a complete isolation but a quest for a different kind of understanding.[168] Turning to oneself can indicate a catatonic apathy of indifference towards the outside, a certain closure of experience, or a socio-pathological passive aggression of withdrawal before attacking.

In opposition to the above-mentioned subjectivist and idealist position of Kristeva based on an inner mirroring, Derrida, in the text accompanying the show *Memoirs of the Blind*, provides

---

163 Roland Barthes, *Roland Barthes*, trans. Richard Howard, London and Basingstoke: Macmillan Press, 1977, p. 41.
164 Sabine Melchior-Bonnet, *The Mirror: A History,* trans. Katherine H. Jewett, London and New York: Routledge, 2006, p. 5. Similarly, Steinberg has defined it as a process; 'I see you see me'. Leo Steinberg, *Velázquez' 'Las Meninas.*
165 He produces a logical twist in which the identity of the subject equals only the self, A=A is negated, as non-A.
166 Julia Kristeva, *Powers of Horror: An Essay on Abjection*, trans. Celine Louis Ferdinand, New York: University of Columbia Press, 1982.
167 Kristeva, *Powers of Horror.*
168 Similarly, Hall notes; 'For Plotinus self-portrait is produced not by looking at a mirror, but withdrawing into the self'. Hall, *The Selfportrait*, p. 19.

a materialist reading of the genre of the self-portrait, denying the idea of self-knowing via the image.[169] Analyzing the paradoxical theme in the discourse of blindness, Derrida focuses on the self-portrait as a mere self-picture, not a self-image.[170] He claims that with self-portraits the author searches for oneself, which is impossible as he is better seen in the real by the Other, as in the myth from ancient Greece. The only possibility of seeing-oneself-seeing is after the accomplishment of the project of self-recording, that would mean; it is only possible to produce portraits of self, never actually to make self-portraits, as it is not possible to see oneself.[171] He continues:

'It is as if the blind man were referring to himself [...], there where a blind Narcissus, inventing a mirror without image, lets it be seen that he does not see. He shows himself, he shows up, but to the other.'[172]

Although writing on graphic arts, etching, and drawing, Jacques Derrida stressed an important element in the cognitive presence of the author; the inclusion of his awareness within the process of etching, which can also be taken for other fine arts.[173] An etcher cannot simultaneously perceive the object sitting in front of him and the paper that he is drawing onto. The author's eye is necessarily shifting and returning back to the paper, occasionally re-constructing viewed scenes, based on a short-time memory.[174] It is in this short time he works on the blind, or as Derrida says; as a blind person, remembering the world once seen, but not experiencing it directly.[175] Or, the etcher can see only the mediated image in the mirror, which is yet another representation, a worn-out mimesis.

This split is well illustrated by a multiple self-portrait by Johannes Gumpp. It is not a real self-portrait, as he represents himself from the back. In this self-portrait, Gumpp is seen from the back, painting his self-portrait at the same time as he is looking at the mirror. Contrary to Jan Vermeer's *Allegory of Painting* (1665-67), also showing a painter from the back, Gumpp provides a description of the action of self-portraying, not providing further information on the way he sees himself from the back. The mirror and the canvas are positioned next to each other, showing no perspectival distortion among themselves, similar to Velázquez's *Las Meninas*. The real figure being represented is obviously imagined, as the painter cannot know how he looks from the back.

169 Exhibition Memoirs of the Blind, Criticizing Ocularcentrism, consisted of 43 drawings, mainly self-portraits, little representation of blindness and one of a ruin. It was presented in the Louvre Museum, 1990-1991.
170 This paradox is clearer distinguishing the self-picture, which a blind person does not have from the kind of self-image they do.
171 Depending on the essence of our existence, we can claim to be able to be at one or two places; to be physically, or to be mentally with the Other. The myth of Narcissus has shown that it is possible to be doubled at once in the wicked universe.
172 Jacques Derrida, *Memoirs of the Blind: The Self-Portrait and Other Ruins*, trans. Pascale-Anne Brault and Michael Naas, Chicago and London: University of Chicago Press, 1993, p. 12.
173 Damisch distinguishes between paintings and mirrors, saying that 'Painting shows, mirror demonstrates,' interpreting Antonio di Pietro Averlino Filarete's idea that in 'specchio ti si demonstra', Damisch deconstructs de-mostra (mostra as exhibition) to emphasize the difference of demonstration and exposition. Damisch, *The Origin of Perspective*.
174 Derrida, *Memoirs of the Blind*.
175 Blindness as an idea was already announced by Bataille's 'Pinneal Eye' in *Story of the Eye*, and based on Freud's idea of visual castration. See: Jay, *Downcast Eyes*, and Georges Bataille, *Story of the Eye*, trans. Dovid Bergelson, Penguin Classics, 2001 (1928).

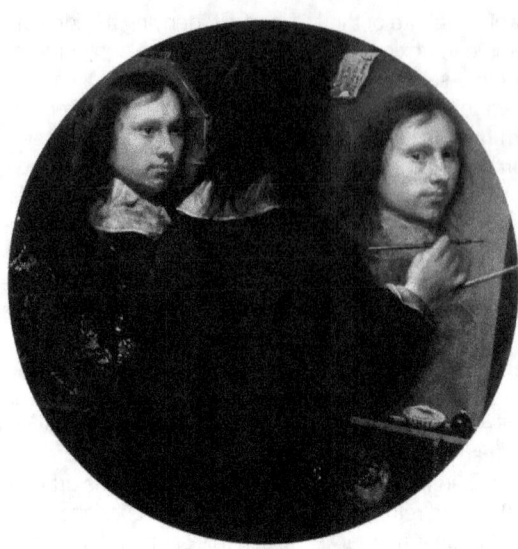

Image 7 – Johannes Gumpp: Self-portrait (1646, Uffizi, Wikimedia, work in the public domain).

The invention of photography, according to Derrida, thus, is twofold.[176] Besides being a technical intervention, photography is also a discovery or a revelation of what is already there, by which it re-invents a definition of the Other. A self-portrait thus would mean inventing the self as the Other. When recording a self-portrait, the photographer is becoming his own object. He objectifies himself, which is actually impossible. To paraphrase Derrida's claim; one can see oneself as being seen, but I can never see myself seeing.[177] And further he noted;

> One thinks that the portrait captures the eyes, the gaze that is, among other things, that for which something like photography [de la photographie] exists. The gaze is presumed to be what the subject himself cannot see in his own life. When one looks at oneself in a mirror, one sees oneself either as seen or as seeing but never as both at the same time. One believes that in principle the camera — photographic or cinematographic — should capture or hold a gaze which the looking eyes cannot see.[178]

Contrary to the media of etching and painting, photography is a medium with an uninterrupted continuity between the object and the subject of the photograph. Speaking in terms of optics, it is the unbroken ray/wave of light allowing and conditioning the viewing process, simultaneously imprinting the image on the film or sensor of the camera. For that capacity, photographic medium was consequently interpreted as a direct imprint of nature onto the film, since the very invention of the medium.[179] This medium is necessarily limited in its objectifying qualities, which, as a consequence, leads to a larger subjectivization of the otherwise objective medium.

176   Jacques Derrida, *Copy, Archive, Signature: A Conversation on Photography,* trans. Jeff fort, Redwood City: Stanford University Press, 2010.
177   Derrida, *Copy, Archive, Signature.*
178   Derrida, *Copy, Archive, Signature,* p. 31.
179   Henry Fox Talbot, *Pencil of Nature,* London: Longman, Brown, Green and Longmans, Project Gutenberg, 2010 (1844).

The Media of Self-Reflection and Self-Storage

Without the photographer, who might as well be the only perceiver of the photograph, an object of the photograph is drawn to a suspicion of its own self-existence. A self-portrait produces a collapse between seeing and gazing of the subject. Although photographic self-portraits look like other photographs, portraits for example, they are just partial sequences. A photograph, moreover, physically occurs halfway between the object and the subject viewing it. It interrupts the ray of light, temporarily freezing the process of viewing, being an integral part of its cognitive presence. As a photographer cannot see both the object and the paper, at once, he cannot be present at both sides of the camera at once.

Media of self-portraits can be distinguished according to their depositing qualities. The proper media of self-reflection are those in which a person sees himself alive. And these are only water, mirror, and mirror-based media. All other media, including drawing, painting and photographs produce a second order reality, serving to store the image into the picture. In drawn, painted, and photographic self-portraits, a painter has to watch him/herself and paint in separate times and space chunks, interrupting the process of self-observation as elaborated by Derrida.[180] Drawings and paintings, but also films, tapes and hard disks, belong more to storage media than to the media of self-reflection.[181] A viewer cannot see himself in the mirror of René Magritte's painting, as painting is not the medium of reflection.[182]

This difference, between the media of self-reflection and storage media, offers a large span of possibilities for intervening, interrupting and interpreting the otherwise straight process of reflection, producing pictures differently than the one originally imaged by the mirroring device as seen in previous examples. And such gap would be resolved in the selfie-culture, which though, by using partially reversible filters and plug-ins, is in nature being continuous. There is no time delay between the performances of seeing and being seen, as with sketching and painting, recording and developing. Contrary to etching and painting, but also some instances of self-portraying photography as I have discussed earlier, selfies do not produce a distraction in the production of the picture. There are no jumps among layers of reality, and continuity forms a perfect loop. A double action is established; recording is seeing while viewing is recording at the same time, with a slight distributive delay. Selfie is immediate and fully controlled. It is possible to see the end result simultaneously while recording.

---

180 Derrida, *Memoirs of the Blind*.

181 In addition to Kittler's storage and broadcast media, another media defines human culture, usually neglected – the media of self-reflection. Kittler distinguishes between media as storage, transmission and processing, defining the revolution of the digital image as the revolution of transmission of image. Friedrich Kittler, *Optical media: Berlin lectures 1999,* trans. Anthony Enns, Cambridge and Walden: Polity, 2010.

182 Finally, the medium of self-reflection can be natural and artificial, single directed and interactive. Memory, water, and mirror are natural, while photography, video, film and web are artificial.

What can be Known are Mere Existentials

Contrary to Derrida's anti-realism regarding self-knowledge, Foucault provides an objectivist account on knowing via the self-image. He provides a historic account on self-knowing, starting with the Greek civilization that introduced both knowing and caring of oneself, to the dominant Catholic society.[183]

One of the paths to distinguish the past relationships to the self from contemporary ones was proposed by Foucault in his lecture titled *Culture of the Self*, to which I also refer in the very title of this book.[184] Foucault defined 'culture of the self' through four important relationships; relationship to us, a critical relationship, authoritarian relationship to the other and practices different from contemplation of the soul.[185] Contemporary culture, being different from the culture of the self, is not fulfilling any demands, according to Foucault.[186] It has no durable relationship to the self, especially not the critical one, nor does it exist in a variety of practices that include others. Still, even such a culture of the self exists as integrated in educational and medical institutions, and the role mass media plays in forming our attitude towards the other.[187]

Although contemporary culture is not one of self-knowledge, it is still characterized by similar preoccupations as the classic culture of self. It continues to be interested in personal self-observation, as for example taking personal notes, conversations and themes for future meditations, now using less classical tools as diaries and letters, but introducing the new mode of the visual diary, also providing a certain care of the self [Gr. *epimeleia heautou*], at least as paying a look at one's own physical state.[188]

---

183 Foucault claims Greco-Roman philosophy distinguished two principles; *epistemesthai satou* from *gnothi saution*, from Socratic dialogues over Xenophon, Hippocrates and Neoplatonic traditions. Christianity as the confessional religion frames a new relationship of the person with the authority, introducing *exomologesis*, a ritual of recognizing oneself as a sinner and penitent. Displaying suffering, shame, humiliation or modesty becomes a norm of exposure of the self, to finally reach the self-revelation, which is the self-destruction as completely obeying and embodying the authority. Since the 16th century, according to Foucault, it is criticism of established morality that has eradicated care of self as an activity of knowing, so in works by Descartes knowing oneself has took the over-important place in philosophy.

184 Michel Foucault, *Culture of the Self*, lectures at UC Berkeley, 1983. Available at: http://www.openculture.com/2014/08/michel-foucaults-lecture-the-culture-of-the-self.html.

185 The lecture introduces the paradigmatic story of Hermotimus from Clazomenae, as told by Greek satirist Lucian of Samosata. Hermotimus had already paid for twenty years for someone to teach him how to care for himself. Still, he is concerned that lectures would demand twenty more years, which is how long they already took, as he is financially drained. Foucault recognizes a full profession after this anecdote, a profession actually paid to explain to others how to love themselves; the philosophers. One of the first, he says, was Socrates, raising question of the care of self, in Plato's *Apology*. Eight centuries later Gregory of Nyssa has also referred the important question, framing the discourse of self. Flourishing of the culture of the self occurred in the 1st and 2nd century, in works by Seneca, Epictetus, Plutarch, Marcus Aurelius, etc. In the lecture, Foucault speaks on notions of care in terms of self-confession in front of a control society, bringing up issues of power relations in regard to our knowledge.

186 Ibid.

187 Foucault, *Culture of the Self*.

188 Foucault notes often contain details of daily lives, quotations and reflections, as, for example, dreams by Aristides. Foucault, *Culture of the Self*.

'Technologies of the Self'[189]

Such self-recording, discussed by Foucault, exists in the selfie culture too. The selfie civilization, in terms of Foucault's conceptualisation of technology of the self, is making an autonomous move onto the care of the self without knowing, as knowing seems to tie it up to the genuine field of morality, ethics, law, and politics.[190] The culture of selfies is visual, rather than literary, and therefore primarily ahistorical, non-narrative and non-critical.

Foucault also suggested that the self should be considered via technologies built through histories, noting that it would be important to see how to elaborate new kinds of relationships with ourselves.[191] Technology produces media as tools of communication and interaction, changing spatiotemporal conditions of the world by new modes of space or time, bridging distances among communication beings or agents of interaction.

Photography, in Foucault's writings, can be seen as both an ontological verifier and epistemic quantifier, allowing knowledge on certain types of existence, usually being focused on peculiarity and uniqueness. Photography not only says that someone exists – this existence is unique and special – it is unrepeatable, for the reasons laid out. Thus, at least two claims that photography stresses can be derived; that someone exists and in a certain way of existence, or as Foucault defines it; 'knowing oneself' is also to 'take care of oneself.'[192]

Such an approach was demonstrated in a diary recorded by Croatian artist Željko Jerman.[193] Jerman's *Moja Godina 1977* was an exhibition coming out as a photographic diary-book, recording a year of his life. Motives for this exhaustive work are announced at the very beginning of the book, and are connected to signalling his existence, by leaving a stable, chemical, trace.[194] On the first of January 1977, he noted:

> "Jerman! do not forget to take a photo of yourself!" since one of the motifs of this work is; even when in a state that you find yourself floating between being and non-being do not forget to work […] always be there, let consciousness conquer the need to deliberate transience in artificial paradise.[195]

Jerman defines an artificial paradise, the paradise of his meta-existence in photographs and texts at the beginning of his yearbook. He states; 'it is primary that this is known by me'

---

189 See: Michel Foucault, 'Technologies of the Self,' in Martin Luther H, Gutman, Patrick H. Hutton (eds.) *Technologies of the Self: A Seminar with Michel Foucault,* Technologies of the Self, London: Tavistock Publications and The University of Massachusetts Press, 1988.

190 In regard to three types of self-examination, being; self-examination with respect to thoughts in correspondence to reality in Descartes, with respect to the way our thoughts relate to rules in Seneca, relation between the hidden thought and inner impurity, Foucault names, it responds to none and that is because Foucauldian system of self-knowing, based on Euclidian geometry as Jones notes, is no longer supported by the media. Jones, 'The 'Eternal Return'.

191 Foucault, *Technologies of the Self.*

192 Foucault, *Technologies of the Self.*

193 Lasch, *The Culture of Narcissism*, p. 48.

194 In general, he is preoccupied with the medium of photography, being looped, presenting self-portraits supplemented with handwritten text. Photographs and portraits appear in equal data sequences, rather than in narrativity of the photographic album. In many logs, he gives reasons for his project – proving his self-existence.

195 Željko Jerman, *Moja godina 1977*, Zagreb: SCCA, 1997, log 1.1.

self-establishing his existence. Self-awareness is not a pre-given, as axiomatic, undoubtable truth, but rather an organic way of monitoring process-awareness, and these processes of self-awareness are in Jerman's case being monitored and recorded on a daily level, in photographs. The 'evidence to the self-existence' is at the same time a connotation of the subject's logical instability in tautology, drawing itself into a magic circle, a tautology claiming; this existence is all that exists, and that is also the purpose of existence.

Work of art, as he defines it, is 'the act of existence affirmation. Its products are existential evidence.'[196] At other places he claims 'The only thing an artist can truly rely on is addressing himself.'[197] Although his life is perfectly described, in terms of events and his own living environment and habits, he still somehow appears lateral and absent from his own photograph, as he is not concentrated on staging and performing at all.[198]

Still, Jerman proves his existence to himself, but also, as he writes, to other people 'that are not that thrilled'.[199] Self-existence is necessarily photographic as it is related to the possibility of seeing one's own body that only photography offers, providing a proof of his existence. But, once a subject becomes his own object, there is no other subject to perceive the object, even the object disappears from any meaningful relationship, which might have previously existed. Maybe that is the most interesting paradox of the self-portrait: its persuasive nature, which has rather a psychological effect than the real's ontological and epistemic power.

The most interesting log in his diary is the log 13.5., where he says; 'I forgot to take a photograph of myself'[200]. But, has he then failed to exist that day? As the diary progresses, Jerman continues to record his own existence, but on this precise day he failed to perceive himself, exist in his self-perceived way. Besides failure, Jerman also describes 'existential neurosis' which is halted by self-recording.[201] According to the entry dated 17.5., it seems he does not remember his own self-recording as it becomes visible he is writing texts and developing photographs with a certain delay. A diary is not simultaneous to events, but rather dependent on time needed for processing of photographic films.[202]

---

196 Jerman, *Moja godina 1977*, log 11.1.

197 Jerman, *Moja godina 1977*, log 16.12.

198 There is a large abyss between the photographic image – often blurred and unfocused to its accompanying text – which is focused and focusing. Image compositions are lateral, as if they are accidental shots. Contrary to latter self-documenting projects, Jerman is not persistent, but rather experimenting both in frame and optical quality of the image, ranging self-images from over-exposed white sheets to under-exposed black area. Images often describe the space, commonly a poor courtyard with a dog and graffiti. We also learn who his mother is, his colleagues and dog, how often he is ill or changes his clothes. Besides, we are introduced to his intimate life details that are not in the picture; as for example when he confesses when was the first time he has been to the theater and a classic concert house.

199 Jerman, *Moja godina 1977*, log 6.1. Subjects seem to have lost their own belief into existence to be urged to claim it and, in case of Jerman, there is also a film he mentions in which he claims his existence by – smoking a cigarette. Jerman, *Moja godina 1977*, log 5.3.

200 Jerman, *Moja godina 1977*, log 13.5.

201 Jerman, *Moja godina 1977*, log 11.7.

202 Which is also visible in a serial of photographs being wrongly developed.

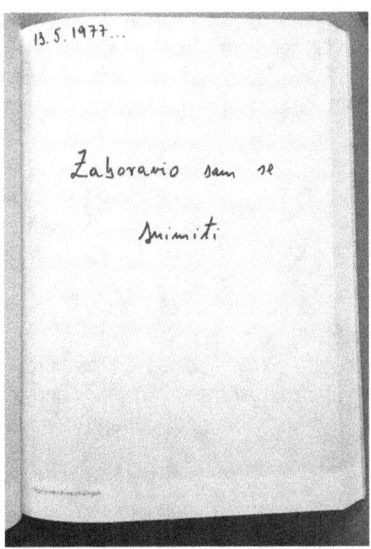

Image 2 – Book page of Željko Jerman: *Moja godina 1977*, log 13.5.

Solipsism and Skepticism in Personal Identity

In Jerman's series of photos, two standpoints of relativism are found; skepticism in mere existence and skepticism in certain qualities of existence, as already mentioned in the discussion on Caravaggio's Narcissus. On the psychological level these two philosophical points speak on the ultimate egotism and problematic instability of the inner self, in which the self-portrait has an important role. According to theories of identity, time inevitably changes personal identity, so self-portraying that captures these changes on the physical level also re-constructs a personal identity, narrating changes, thus building a 'narrative self,' a self that is told through time, but on which narration can follow-up even the disappearance of the self (and at that place, precisely, photography stands for; a memento).[203] Exposing such portraits is there to question but also guarantee a person's existence in time and space, as well as the person's continuity on an external, public timeline.

Madness of Self-Imaging

Documentation of past appearances, agglomerating in the archive of self-portraits, constructing a narrative historical self, is constantly updated with self-insights into changes a human face undergoes while aging. Each of 'the last' self-portraits denies the spectacularity of the effect of aging from the previous one. Facing aging has also become a part of the new time philosophy, which arises as a consequence of visuality of the self-portrait, a phenomenon of recording the self to prove one's existence on a time line. As 'special moments' in which a person's self-records proliferate, so does the insecurity of one's own existence.

---

203 Like the concept employed by Greenblatt. Stephen Greenblatt, *Renaissance Self-fashioning*, Chicago: University of Chicago Press, 1980.

Besides existence, photography was used to express states it cannot directly capture; emotions, behavioral and psychological disorders. In general, the mode of mystification and psychologization of the late 19th and early 20th century, photography was pushed to record what was generally used for stigmatization of madness as general symptom, rather than any diagnosis.

Madness was attributed to self-images in narratives appearing already in ancient Greek culture, believing one dies on seeing one's own reflection. Aristotle himself constructed a theory of a 'bloody mirror,' a mirror stained by the gaze of a menstruating woman.[204] The capacity of the mirror to produce madness has been emphasized by its curved shape, distorting the presentation, and, according to some, influencing the madness, as described in the *Ship of Fools* novel by Sebastian Brant, giving a place to the mirror for seeing who they are.[205] Medieval, paranoiac beliefs that the Evil resides inside the mirror defined it a tool of the Devil, characterized by its reflexivity and mimicry, and by its illusionary, negative space of the world behind. They reached a peak in the character of Dorian Gray, cursing the picture to have the life he himself deserved.[206]

Stabilizing the mirrored image, photography evolved since the beginning of both clinical psychiatry and psychotherapy, where it was employed or maybe has even given the impetus to cruel practices characteristic of the 19th century. It doesn't appear as a marginal fact that introspection as a method was introduced in the same century that invented technologies of image recording.[207] Photography and psychoanalysis were for long overlapping fields, on the technical level conditioning perceptions with image repetition, framing and cropping of reality, while on the theoretical side introducing new focuses of necrophilia, voyeurism and fetishism as consequences of development of the medium.[208]

Besides, photography served as an explanation paradigm, succeeding the model of camera obscura, taken as a reference to the subconscious. In *The Interpretation of Dreams*, Freud has compared the psyche to a visual tool resembling a microscope or a photographic apparatus.[209] Although concerned with the portrait, writing in *Notes on Faces and Man* for

---

204 Aristotle in De Insomnis: 'That the sensory organs are acutely sensitive to even a slight qualitative difference [in their objects] is shown by what happens in the case of mirrors; a subject to which, even taking it independently, one might devote close consideration and inquiry. [...] If a woman chances during her menstrual period to look into a highly-polished mirror, the surface of it will grow cloudy with a blood-coloured haze. It is very hard to remove this stain from a new mirror, but easier to remove from an older mirror.' Aristotle, *On Dreams*, http://classics.mit.edu/Aristotle/dreams.html.

205 See: Sebastian Brant, S. *Ship of Fools*, New York: Dover Publications, 2011 (1494), p. 59.
     Another interesting character, Alice, enters the crazy land behind the looking glass in Carroll's *Through the Looking Glass*. This narrative carries certain horror elements as la *folie du logis*: Red Queen behaves as in psychiatric asylum, from which Alice cannot escape till Alice's awakening from the hallucination. In Martin Gardner, *The Annotated Alice. Alice's Adventures in Wonderland and Through the Looking Glass* by Lewis Carroll – intro and notes Martin Gardner, Wing Books, 1993 (1960).

206 See; also Melchior-Bonnet claiming mirror and madness share the capacity of mystification. Melchior-Bonnet, *The Mirror*, p. 199.

207 Wilhelm Wundt, 1879 Cca.

208 Bergstein is concerned with destruction of portraits, burning photographs and similar magical practices developed in Europe. See: Mary Bergstein, *Mirrors of Memory: Freud, Photography and the History of Art*, Ithaca and London: Cornell University Press, 2010.

209 Freud assumed that every mental process exists to begin with in an unconscious stage or phase and that it is only from there that the process passes over into the conscious phase, just as a photographic

the National Portrait Gallery, Freud still hasn't researched photography deeply, although his theories might have been well influenced by the photographic medium. According to Mary Bergstein photography as a medium might have influenced the development of different theories of Freudian analysis, such as; fetishism, magical thinking, surrogacy and animism.[210] So she concluded; 'If psychoanalysis was a methodology for seeing into the past and collapsing time, so was photography.'[211]

Similarly, Walter Benjamin compared the camera to the subconscious in his *Small History of Photography*; 'The camera introduces us to unconscious optics as does psychoanalysis to unconscious impulses.'[212] Benjamin further elaborated the thesis of photography as a metaphor of the unconscious, introducing the concept of the optical unconscious in photography, while saying that photography is similar to psychoanalysis,[213] Rosalind E. Krauss, in her fragmented theory of *The Optical Unconscious,* continued using the concept in the original, for the analysis of surreal and abstract pieces of art.[214] But the hidden, oppressed, and fragmented self belongs to the period succeeding Benjamin's writings. So, to understand the practice of mirror-transference in self-portraiture, a deeper relationship of photography to psychoanalysis has to be uncovered.[215]

In practice, one research, carried out with the use of photography, had played a particular role in the development of modern psychiatry. Jean-Martin Charcot, a pupil of Guillaume Duchenne de Boulogne, orientated to externally record inner states, used photographs in diagnostics at the Salpêtriere sanatorium and became known for images of hysteria and hypnosis.[216] Charcot has used photography to diagnose what he named small and large

picture begins as a negative and only becomes a picture after being formed into a positive. Not every negative, however, necessarily becomes a positive; nor is it necessary that every unconscious mental process should turn into a conscious one. This may be advantageously expressed by saying that an individual process belongs to begin with to the system of the unconscious and can then, in certain circumstances, pass over into the system of the conscious.' Sigmund Freud: The Standard Edition of the Complete Psychological Works of Sigmund Freud: *Introductory lectures on psycho-analysis*, pt. III, Hogarth Press and the Institute of Psycho-Analysis, 1963, p. 295.

210 Bergstein, *Mirrors of Memory*.
211 Bergstein, *Mirrors of Memory*, p. 23.
212 Walter Benjamin, *The Work of Art in the Age of Mechanical Reproduction*. Francis Frascina, Charles Harrison et al. (eds.) *Modern Art and Modernism, a Critical Anthology,* London: Paul Chapman & Open University, 1982 (1936), p. 203.
213 Rosalind Krauss, *Optical Unconsciousness*, Cambridge: MIT Press, 1993.
214 Krauss notes; 'My own use of optical unconscious, as it has been invoked in the pages of this book, is thus at an angle in Benjamin's Krauss, *Optical Unconsciousness*, p. 129.
215 Lacan's metaphor of the mirror-stage has been widely deployed by a number of psychotherapists, as for example Kohut, who further defined the forms of mirror transference. Kohut has discussed treatments of narcissism in Kohut; 'The Psychoanalytic Treatment of Narcissistic Personality Disorders' (1968). Today, theory is assumed under the theory of mirror neurons developed by Galese who has conducted experiments using magnetic resonance, which have proven that both monkeys and humans have mirror neurons helping them in emphatic relationship towards others. See: Vittorio Gallese and Al Goldman 'Mirror neurons and the simulation theory of mind reading', *Trends in Cognitive Sciences* 12.2 (1998).
216 French neurologist Guilliaume Duchenne de Boulogne back in 1862, was the first one experimenting with recording of psychic conditions induced by electro-shocks, thus founding electrophysiology. The method he described in the essay *Album de Photographies Pathologiques Complementaire du Livre Intitule 'De l'electrisation localisee.'* Duchenne's use was often seen as innovative and creative, but also criticized as radically sadistic.

hysteria [Lat. *hysteria minor, hysteria major*], both present in female populations.[217] These naively staged pictures of exalted women were made to certify the diagnosis, rather than to show a power of expression in photographic portraits in general. It is no wonder Freud was also studying at the Salpêtriere hospital, which could have influenced the visual layout of psychoanalytical theory, as described earlier.[218] Freud, Jewish himself, has been interested in the Salpêtriere research in particular, for the reason that it was grounded in photogrammetry and later the mode of eugenics which informed the photographic archives, preceded by Duchenne de Boulogne's approaches, according to Bergstein.[219] Although pushed by their research, contemporary implementation of photography into psychotherapy has little to do with physiognomic experiments by Duchenne or Charcot, or even Alphonse Bertillon, Cesare Lombroso and Francis Galton.[220]

Its later implementations ranging from diagnostics and care, but also the amortization of self-maintenance and self-care in the recent age, had psycho-therapeutic mirror-transference theories resonating in its background. Visual media has been advised as a therapeutic tool since the 70s, around the peak of the self-portrait genre. Clinical photo-therapy, as a method developed by Raymond Cornelison, in the 60s, was set in practice only by the 70s by a number of therapists in Canada, UK and USA.[221] Its goal was not set towards diagnostics, but rather assistance using photography as a combined therapeutic tool.[222] Besides, photography can be engaged in self-analysis.[223] Photo-therapeutic centers use a variety of photographic methods and practices to research, explore and interpret one's relationship to reality, such as; photographing, photo-editing, analysis and discussing pictures, presenting

---

217 Georges Didi-Huberman, *Invention of Hysteria: Charcot and the Photographic Iconography of the Salpêtrière*, trans. Alisa Hartz, Cambridge and London: MIT Press, 2003.

218 Charcot, with his team Paul Richer, Gilles de la Tourette, Albert Londe and Paul Regnard recorded different symptoms Bergstein described as 'scorn, menace, paralysis, mockery or amorous supplication'. Bergstein, *Mirrors of Memory*, p. 78.
     These works were published as *L'iconographie photographique de la Salpêtrière* (1876-80). Still, as Didi Huberman reported, photographs produced in the Salpêtriere hospital, were rather constructions of the photographic evidence of the malady of hysteria. Georges Didi-Huberman, *Invention of Hysteria: Charcot and the Photographic Iconography of the Salpêtrière*, trans. Alisa Hartz, Cambridge and London: MIT Press, 2003.

219 Built by Cesare Lombroso, Alphonse Bertillon, and Francis Galton, eugenics presented unification of appearances needed for the medical diagnostics. Bergstein, *Mirrors of Memory*.

220 Sekula states this type of photograph leads to a segregation of society, onto criminals and ones that are not, but also of new administration. New taxonomic applications of photography, like physiognomy and phrenology, lead to a development of criminology as a discipline. See: Allan Sekula, 'The Body and the Archive', *October* 39 (Winter, 1986).

221 Doug Stewart, Judy Weiser, David Krauss and Joel Walker are considered to be fathers FIX of the phototherapy practice. In the UK, Art and Drama teacher Keith Kennedy, working in Hederson Psychiatric Hospital founded a 'group camera' practice, also collaborating with the artist Jo Spence.

222 Halkola defines principal aims to use photographs in psychotherapy as; 'impulses to memory and to recognizing and expressing emotions, thus promoting the self-understanding of the client. It is a question of a comprehensive process where the photos used in therapy are connected to the client's mental images, beliefs and memories of self. The event of viewing or taking photos evokes sensations, emotions and memories, which can be of a very early, painful or surprising nature.' Halkola via Del Loewenthal (ed) *Phototherapy and Therapeutic Photography in a Digital Age*, London and New York: Routledge, 2013, p. 21.

223 Elena Nedelcu and Andra Nedelcu, 'The Exploration of the Self in Pictures: Photo-Therapy', *Challenges of the Knowledge Society. Social sciences* 25 (2012).

old pictures, exhibiting, writing and captioning, constructing photo albums or photo books.[224] New developments of photo-therapy moved towards research in the exact sciences, such as neuroscience.[225] Other, supplementary methods were developed since, especially with digital media, researching capacities of digital imagery in preventing and curing different psychological problems.

Photo-therapy proved to be advantageous to general, healthy, populations, influencing their self-esteem.[226] Photography-assisted therapy has also been explored with patients who have experienced different types of traumas. Photography proved to be beneficial in cases where patients were unable or unwilling to speak about their trauma, as for example with child abuse. Photographs shown were useful tools in situations and conditions in which patients were unable to self-formulate, either for the reason of lack of vocabulary in general, or the shortage of precise expressions suitable for verbalizing different states or feelings, or finally in situations of socially conditioned self-censorship, prohibiting a conscious direct speech. For the same reasons, photographs are useful in therapies with disadvantaged people and children patients. Besides as expression, photography is used as memento and as memory, shown in order to aid memories in treatment of Alzheimer or PTSD, according to Simone Alter-Muri.[227]

Self-portrait plays a crucial role in phototherapy.[228] Judy Weiser noted;

'Self-Portrait Photo-Therapy work can help clients clarify their self-images and raise their self-esteem and self-confidence through making, viewing, and accepting images of themselves and owning their positive perceptions'.[229]

Some psychotherapy practices are deepening the cultural concepts of auto-photography and self-exploration.[230] Still, in general, although detailed in descriptions and used in practice, photo-therapists' insight into phototherapy do not offer much on the general reading that would be crucial for the insight into self-therapeutic use of photography, besides terms of self-therapy, as for example provided by Nuñez.[231]

---

224 Therapeutic Photography, https://phototherapy-centre.com/therapeutic-photography/.

225 Karlsson in Del Loewenthal, *Phototherapy and Therapeutic Photography in a Digital Age*, p. 162. The hypothesis of Eric Kandel states psychotherapy leads to changes in gene expression through learning, by altering strength of synaptic connections between nerve cells and inducing morphological changes in neurons.

226 Carrey M. Noland, 'Auto-Photography as Research Practice: Identity and Self-Esteem Research', *Journal of Research Practice* 2.1 (2006).

227 Simone Alter-Muri, Beyond the Face: Art Therapy and Portraiture, *The Arts in Psychotherapy* 34 (2007).

228 Cristina Nuñez, 'The Self Portrait, a Powerful Tool for Self-Therapy, *European Journal of Psychotherapy & Counselling* 11 (2009): 51-61, DOI: 13642530902723157.
     Weiser defined five photographic techniques used in psychotherapy; the projective process, implementing photographs to explore patient's perceptions, values and expectations, working with self-portraits, analyzing portraitists of self-made by others, and using photographs as metaphors of self-construction collected by patient and building photo-systems. Del Loewenthal, *Phototherapy and Therapeutic Photography in a Digital*, p. 6.

229 Weiser in Del Loewenthal, *Phototherapy and Therapeutic Photography in a Digital Age*, p. 130.

230 Cristina Nuñez, 'The Self Portrait, a Powerful Tool for Self-Therapy', *European Journal of Psychotherapy & Counselling* 11 (2009); and Elena Nedelcu and Andra Nedelcu, 'The Exploration of the Self in Pictures: Photo-Therapy', *Challenges of the Knowledge Society. Social sciences* 25 (2012).

231 Nuñez, *The Self Portrait.*

Between Moodiness and Madness

Even previous to the development of art therapy, many artists recorded their own psychic state. Courbet has left us a series of images showing himself without any self-control. In *Desperate Man* (1845) he recorded his own suicide in a picture, acting like he is out of control. Besides mood swings, consequential recordings of 'getting mad' were painted by Vincent van Gogh and Frida Kahlo, and sculpted by Franz Xaver Messerschmidt.[232]

Many of the self-portraying photographs are rather embodiments of the idea, than representations of the self, as was already analyzed in the paradoxical first self-portrait of Hippolyte Bayard. Fortunato Depero was one of the first artists who tried to analyze inauthentic emotion in his grimaces. Feminist artist Wilke produced the video *Gestures* (1975) that shows in a minimalist visual setup, hands modeling a face, up to the smile.[233] Similarly, Sanja Iveković, in her *Instructions* (1976) has referred to the ideal face. Both Wilke and Iveković deconstructed their own self-control and posed in desirable modes, as women, but also as objects of a chauvinist gaze, who have to smile in a man-ruled world.

Besides directly communicating with the public, some self-portraits forward messages of emotional and soul states, conditioning the emotional response of the public.[234] Although not as systematically as contemporary selfie projects, recording self-expressions by the camera were already being practiced by a Dutch visual artist, Bas Jan Ader, and other authors working with transgression, like Ron Athey, provoking similar reactions from the public. Ader has recorded various states of depression, while Athey recorded self-aggressions on his own body. In cases such as Ader, pictures sent out were screams for help, while in cases of Van Gogh and Kahlo they were tools for self-researching. Similarly, some less famous artists have fully documented their illness, as for example William Utermohlen who recorded his fall into Alzheimer's disease, or Bryan Saunders who recorded changes in his own psychic conditions when taking different drugs.

One of the first self-therapeutic cycle of self-analysis, but also self-recalling, is Anne Noggle's photo-series of herself recovering from a face-lift in 1975. Still, an artist who is credited for developing the phototherapy is Jo Spence, diagnosed with breast cancer and afterwards leukemia.[235] Spence recorded her own illness in a series, *Cancer shock* (1982), as well as

---

232 Some modern painters taking self-portraits were diagnosed with manic depression, maybe the most prominent examples of Modernist self-reference are Van Gogh's portraits, sent to his brother, along with letters that were evidence of the condition of a painter inside the asylum. He would supplement his reports to his brother with self-portraits. Maybe the best-known clinical examples of self-portraying in painting was that of Brian Charnley, a painter suffering from schizophrenia.
Hugh J. Silverman, 'Cezanne's Mirror Phase' in Galen A. Johnson (ed) The Merleau-Ponty, *Aesthetics Reader: Philosophy and Painting*, Evanston: Northwestern University Press, 1993.

233 Part of the video can be seen on Youtube: https://www.youtube.com/watch?v=FLSfemMX6tE.

234 As for example Rebecca Brown, suffering from trichotillomania. See: 'She Took a Daily Selfie While Battling Depression – Here is the Result', Wimp, https://youtu.be/eRvk5UQY1Js.

235 Spence started a Re-enactment Photo Therapy in collaboration with Rosy Martin, later summing up her theses on therapy via photography (Martin, 2009). She defined re-enactment phototherapy, using mirrors, presented as a show *Remodelling Photo History*. 'Making visible process, change and transformation, by going to the source of an issue or an old trauma, re-enacting it and making a new ending; a new possibility.' Martin, 2009: 41. Jo Spence and Rosy Martin organized photo-therapeutic family sessions, in which families staged dramatic inner relationships to the camera. For developing

in another named *The Picture of Health* (1982-6), continuing to follow developments to the last, simply named *Final project* (1992). One of the most striking images she has produced is the self-portrait recorded near the grave, being a part of the *Final project* facing near death.[236] In the picture, she stands over the grave-hole dug in the ground, looking down into it, facing the abyss.

Wilke, mentioned above for her *Grimaces* video, also recorded illness and death, starting with photographs of her mother dying of breast cancer, but later also her struggle with the illness, and chemotherapy, in a series of photographs entitled *Intra-Venus* (1982). Wilke's work bridges photography and performance art in her self-portraits, which seems to have inspired the whole theme of 'performing identity,' based on psychoanalysis.[237] Only with feminist photography's introduction of the vulnerable self into the public domain, done by screening on a surface the subconscious of the portrayed person, art therapy is fully advocated.

That there are differences among self-photographing in the 80s and today is clear once we compare photographs from both times, for example Hannah Wilke's hospital self-portrait with the hospital selfie from The Selfie Olympics.[238] Wilke's work, in general, was focused on her illness throughout. Most of it is very sad and depressing, asking for care and gentleness, as well as recognition of topics which appear as taboo; trauma of the operation, malignant diseases which are not diagnosed in time because of cultural taboos, as well as experiences of a woman who has been operated upon in a world that always demanded youth and beauty.

Contrary to Wilke, the hospital selfie shows a lady with a self-flattering attitude, and was probably having a nicer day than many of people watching the photograph for some reason. But, the question is: is she just prettier or does she want to look prettier to the public? Is her self-image directed by a desirable projection, or is it real? And finally, is she happy because the illness is gone?

---

various techniques and methods of phototherapy, today Spence is considered a founder of method and the most prominent example of almost heroic act of dealing with trauma, with the use of this technological mirror. Spence defined the therapy: 'Instead of fixity, to us it represents a range of possibilities which can be brought into play at will, examined, questioned, accepted, transformed, discarded. Drawing on techniques learned from co-counseling, psycho-drama and the reframing technique we began to work together to give ourselves and each other permission to display 'new' visual selves to the camera.' http://selfportrait-experience.com/. For more on Jo Spence see: http://www.jospence.org/.

236 See: http://www.jospence.org/final_project/f_p_3.html.

237 Tamar Tembeck, 'Exposed Wounds, The Photographic Autopathographies of Hannah Wilke and Jo Spence', *RACAR* XXXIII (2008). Assisted self-portraits as those of Rosy Martin helping Jo Spence to self-portray, or Donald Goddard assisting Hannah Wilke are not common though they are practiced today too. This practice has reached the paradoxical point in self-portraits of contemporary artists, such as Jemma Stehli, whose self-portrait show a man deciding on shooting the image, during her stripping performance, or in Slater Bradley's portrait in which he has a doppelganger who acts as him performing others.

238 See: https://jesleen92.files.wordpress.com/2014/03/cancer-selfie.jpg.

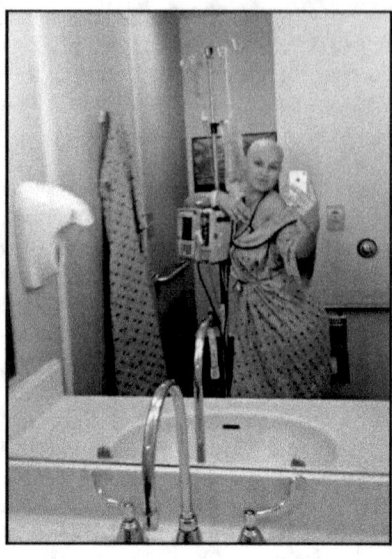

Image 9 – Hospital selfie, Selfie Olympics (2014).

Medical and Judgmental Gaze

A difference between artists dealing with therapy and real psychotherapists using art as a tool, is in the presence of the public and the participation of the gaze of the psychotherapist inside the process of objectification of the self, of becoming subject, as contrary to subjectivization of the self as an object. Art therapy is centered on the self as an ultimate public and receiver of the objectified self-message, contrary to online public alternatives of self-therapies, such as forums, addressing an unknown public and foreseeing unpredictable consequences. A recent case of a woman who by undressing on Facebook to show her operation scars from a serious illness that she was recovering, from lost Facebook 'friends' instantly, as a consequence of this public stripping.[239] Depending on whether her motive was to present herself as she was, or how she thought she was, or if she wanted merely to be accepted as she was, the results may be both healing and fatal to, her already vulnerable, self-esteem.

---

239 Beth-Whaanga's photograph of herself in a red dress and naked, displaying scars. Whaanga posed to photographer Nadia Masot after having double mastectomy. Ryan Lippman, 'Beth Waanga shows her cancer scars on Facebook', *Daily Mail*, 12 February 2014, http://www.dailymail.co.uk/news/article-2557244/Beth-Whaanga-shows-cancer-scars-Facebook. Mastectomy Pictures: http://www.huffingtonpost.co.uk/rebecca-sparrow-/mastectomy-pictures_b_4781776.html.

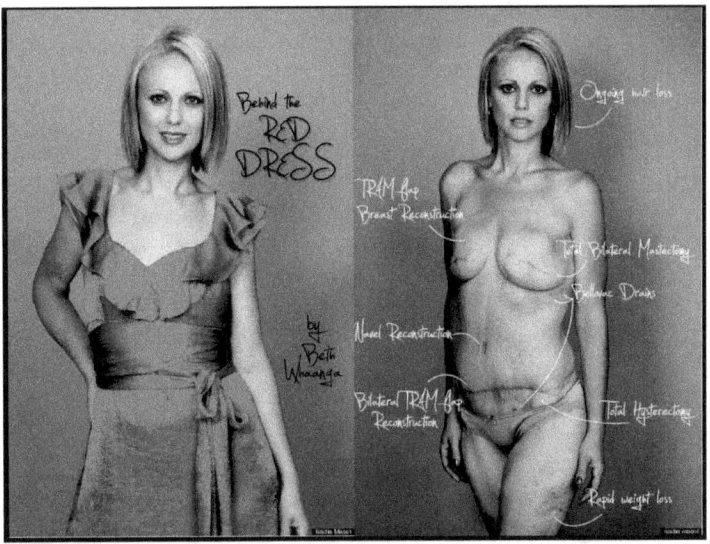

Image 10 – Beth-Whaanga and Nadia Massot: *Under the Red Dress* (2014).

Readers tend to project their own emotions onto photographs of others, which has been shown in studies on depression. Simultaneously, all the possible readings of the same image, including the author's own reading would be based on empathy. So, it makes a big difference if her self-portrait is projecting her own medical, i.e. therapeutic gaze onto the public or if the public is absorbing her self-portrait with a judgmental gaze. Two gazes in the contemporary age can be traced back to a long tradition, one started with the epistemological turn succeeding successful autopsies, during the times of Marie François Xavier Bichat, who contributed to developing the medical profession while sadistically enjoying public dissections of bodies of criminals, and the other being a complex social phenomena of rising middle class of 19th century.[240] Elisabeth Klaver defines the medical gaze after Foucault's formulation of the 'piercing gaze': 'The medical gaze would be able to recognize the body as a vertical and horizontal terrain as it "plunges," "penetrates," "advances," and "descends" (Foucault's verbs) into ever deeper and stratified space.'[241] Therapeutic gaze is commonly defined as part of a medical professional judgment or diagnosis and therapy.[242] Outcomes of therapeutic selfies are, thus, unpredictable, as it is impossible to forecast which type of the gaze would change the reception and meaning of the self-portrait in the public sphere; therapeutic, medical, judgmental, chauvinistic, or even sadistic. The judgmental gaze, contrary to the medical one

---

240 Elisabeth Klaver, *Sites of Autopsy in Contemporary Culture*, New York, SUNY Series in Postmodern Culture, 2005.

241 Klaver, *Sites of Autopsy in Contemporary Culture*, p. 18.

242 Heidi Rimke, 'The Culture of Therapy: Psychocentrism in Everyday Life', in M. Thomas (ed.) *Power and Everyday Practices*, Toronto: Nelson, 2012, pp. 182-202. Rimke defines therapeutic gaze by the need for self-enlightenment; 'We are incited to seek self-enlightenment by excavating and exposing our 'true' selves to the therapeutic gaze in multiple forms, such as our MSN friends, online diagnostic questionnaires, Facebook applications, or fashion magazine quizzes.' Heidi Rimke, *The Culture of Therapy*, p. 194.

is defined only recently, by feminist critique, as for example by Mosher.[243] The judgmental attitude, characterized by a lack of knowledge and overload of attitude represents a social condemning of certain appearances, as fat, dirty, anorexic bodies, ugly, sick, or dead bodies, not even sparing corpses.

Amateur Self-Therapy

Our contemporary age is being framed by a chronic need of the assistance of the psychiatrist. According to McLuhan we live in the Age of Anxiety.[244] In contemporary, mediated society, people are willing to abandon their own cages while still being usable, migrating safely into virtual bodies, liberating themselves from pain, death and decay of physical body, as Narcissus seems to have done.[245]

While for McLuhan there is nothing wrong with the mediation of Narcissus, individual and social psychosomatics of the 20th century has rather condemned it.[246] Narcissism of con-temporary society is connected to self-help phenomena, Lasch has recorded; 'The new narcissist is haunted not by guilt but by anxiety.'[247] He saw 'contemporary climate is therapeutic, not religious' providing thus a ground for the interpretation of self-help culture rising in 70s and growing since.[248] That culture tends to the proliferation of psychiatric modes of thought, Lasch concluded.[249]

From Lacan on, ethical considerations in the global teaching and promotion of art therapy to non-art therapists, gained importance, as explained by Kalmanowitz and Potash.[250] Today's internet society promotes a variety of cheap replacements for expensive medicine, raising a paranoia about medicine, based on the argument that it is connected to the rapid development of the pharmaceutical industry, which exclusive goal is profit, not humanitarianism. While photo-therapy was promoted as a cure by real professionals in the field in the 80s, now it is promoted on DIY sites as a must-do activity.[251]

---

243 Michael A. Mosher, 'The Judgmental Gaze of European Women: Gender, Sexuality, and the Critique of Republican Rule', *Political Theory* 22 (1994).

244 Marshall McLuhan, *Understanding Media*.

245 It is interesting to compare definitions of media body reference, as for example in Belting, who claims that on the perceptive level, as media also inscribes body experience it is plausible to analyze media as body. He says; 'The notion that pictures are images embodied in media brings out body, a living medium of its own, back into the discussion.' Hans Belting, *An Anthropology of Images, Picture, Medium*, Body, Princeton and Oxford: Princeton University Press, 2011, p. 11.

246 Since of DSM-5, narcissism is not proposed not to be taken as a distinct disorder any more. See: *DSM-5: Proposed Revisions: Personality and Personality Disorders'*, American Psychiatric Association, (2010).

247 Lasch, *The Culture of Narcissism*, p. XVI.

248 Lasch, *The Culture of Narcissism*, p. 7. This, contemporary spiritualism reviews and exploits good effects of narcissism. See also: Ann Gleig, 'The Culture of Narcissism Revised, Transformations of Narcissism in Contemporary Psychospirituality', *Pastoral Psychology* 59 (2010), DOI: 10.1007/s11089-009-027-9.

249 Expanding Jim Hougan's thesis that 'The anxieties at the Middle Ages are not much different than those of the present. Then as now, social upheaval gave rise to 'millenarian sects'. Lasch, *Culture of Narcissism*, p. 4.

250 Kalmanowitz and Potash, 'Ethical considerations in the global teaching and promotion of art therapy to non-art therapists', *The Arts in Psychotherapy* 37 (2010): 20-26.

251 Amateurism is not a recent phenomenon, it had started already with the disappearance of arts and

Even though photo-therapy is recommended for self-use even by professionals, there are some dangers in freely employing it.[252] Besides professionals, numerous non-professionals offer treatments with alternative methods.[253] In some cases, it can be rather dangerous to allow amateurs to conduct therapies. Muri claims it is not necessary that self-run projects will help, especially in regard to maladies such as depression, as they can enforce negative thinking, obsessive disorders, as well as they can amplify repetitive patterns.[254] A self-preoccupation can, moreover, deepen the loss of self in schizophrenia, an illness in which a patient cannot clearly distinguish oneself from the environment, as a patient does not have ego boundaries, but is at the same time preoccupied with oneself.[255] Obsessive self-portraying can amplify certain aspects of depression, as for example, building up a negative self-image, drowning a person deeper into the abyss of despair. It can also intensify a bipolar disorder, especially in the phase of inflated self-esteem, leading to uncontrollable behavior.[256] It can enforce alienation from communication, by attaching attention to the process of recording. Furthermore, it can enforce dissociation, the ability to integrate all the components of self into a coherent representation of one's identity. Finally, such phototherapy can raise enormous frustrations with regard to digital acceptance, such as the number of 'likes' or followers in Narcissist mid-life crisis, as already mentioned.[257] So, a person engaging in processes of self-recording has to be extremely cautious, being able to recognize the exact moment when to ask for a second opinion or more professional help.[258]

crafts at the last stage of 'capitalism with limited responsibility' in which even the responsibility to know to be able to offer the service completely failed. Many professions become less exclusive; photographers among others too, being overtaken by industries or larger companies in which non-professionals was employed... 'User based capitalism' almost completely erased tourist agencies, PR agencies. The profession of the photographer was one of the first to disappear, on amateur sites offering low-cost or royalty-free photographs on image stock platforms, starting with Getty images to Shutterstock, pushing out of the market professional advertising and product photographers, press photographers, but also photographic agencies.

252 Natalie R. Carlton, 'Digital culture and art therapy', The Arts in Psychotherapy 41 (2014): 41-45.

253 Debra Kalmanowitz and Jordan S. Potash, 'Ethical considerations in the global teaching and promotion of art therapy to non-art therapists', The Arts in Psychotherapy 37 (2010).

254 Simone Alter-Muri, 'Beyond the Face: Art therapy and Portraiture', The Arts in Psychotherapy 34 (2007).

255 Louis A. Sass, 'Introspection, Schizophrenia, and the Fragmentation of Self Representations', Representations 19 (1987).

256 Ibid.

257 See also: Natalie R. Carlton, Digital culture and art therapy.

258 The reason why a scam claiming that the American Psychological Association recognized selfie as a tool of self-destruction, and that selfitis is a disease of inflammation of ones' ego worked, was precisely for the common sense that it presented.

V. IN THE MIRROR OF PERSEUS

In our time, we expect that the death of public persona will be a media event. The picture of the deceased is meant to introduce the dead in their new (only pictorial) status.[259]

'Greetings From the Concentration Camp'

One of the most radical and perpetual transgressions in the contemporary culture of the selfie is the presentation of death. An interesting case, dating back to early 2014, is the case of a girl named Breanna Mitchell from Alabama. Her smiling selfie recorded at the Nazi camp in Auschwitz, Poland, fell into the hands of the media of 'the global village'.[260] In the picture, that shortly went viral, Breanna, dressed in a pink shirt, smiled in front of two campus main buildings. Numerous portals reported on a public lynching succeeding the release of the picture.[261] Breanna was heavily bullied and even threatened with death, she claimed.[262] Finally, pressured by the public, she revealed motives lying behind the recording, by a personal confession, retelling a very intimate narrative, a sad story of her own personal loss behind the act of self-picturing.[263]

Two years after the controversial Auschwitz selfie, plenty of selfies at places of commemoration and death have followed. Even more disputable pictures are recorded at sites of execution or individual death events and sermons, posing with dying people in hospitals, at funerals, memorials, or even with exhumed cadavers. One of these funeral selfies depicts a smiling person in front of a coffin of a deceased older Afro-American lady, in another smiling self-portrait, a lady with a corpse is seen with an autopsy displayed behind her back. Photographing at funerals has become a common practice. According to the *Daily Mail*, recording selfies at funerals and memorial sites, such as concentration camps or the 9/11 Memorial, has become a fashion in itself. Among famous figures taking them, there are also many public figures, such as former US President Obama who took a selfie at Nelson Mandela's memorial.[264] A

259 Hans Belting, *An Anthropology of Images, Picture, Medium, Body*, Princeton and Oxford: Princeton University Press, 2011, p. 3.
260 '"I wouldnt do anything differently": Teen who took selfie at Auschwitz is unrepentant as trend for grinning and pouting poses at memorials including Ground Zero grows', *Daily Mail*, 23 July 2014, http://www.dailymail.co.uk/news/article-2702161/I-wouldnt-differently-Teenager-took-selfie-Auschwitz-unrepentant-trend-posing-memorials-including-Ground-Zero-grows.html.
261 Daily Mail Online, NY Daily News, Washington Post, The Huffington Post... et.al.
262 Lee Moran, 'Alabama girl gets death threads after taking selfie at Auschwitz', *NY Daily News*, 25 July 2014, http://www.nydailynews.com/news/national/alabama-girl-death-threats-selfie-auschwitz-article-1.1879908.
263 Caitlin Dewey, 'The Other Side of Infamous Auschwitz Selfie', *Washington Post*, 22 July 2014, https://www.washingtonpost.com/news/the-intersect/wp/2014/07/22/the-other-side-of-the-infamous-auschwitz-selfie/. Jessica Durando, 'Auschwitz Selfie Girl Defends Her Action', *USA Today*, 23 July 2014, https://www.usatoday.com/story/news/nation-now/2014/07/23/selfie-auschwitz-concentration-camp-germany/13038281/. Jessica Durando, 'Auschwitz Selfie Girl Breanna Mitchell Defends Her Controversial Picture', *The Huffington Post*, 24 July 2014, http://www.huffingtonpost.com/2014/07/24/auschwitz-selfie-girl-breanna-mitchell_n_5618225.html.
264 See for example; Cheryl K. Chumley and Dave Boyer, 'Obama takes selfie at Mandela's funeral service',

new genre in photography, more precisely self-photography is a #darkselfie, having its sub-genres in a #funeralselfie, #hospital selfie etc.

The Culture of Dissection[265]

Images of dead people are surely not new to our visual culture, still, there are different traditions of representation, ranging from symbolic to the super-real. Death in news is commonly broadcasted as cold, immobile, frozen and stiff, but still – hardly ever decaying, contrary to, for example, bodies depicted in forensic photographic practice. Forensic documentations, made by pathologists, police officers or coroners, recording a biological or medical condition of the body after death, are commonly made for internal, institutional purposes of analysis. These images present cadavers in the way we do not want to see them, at various stages of decay.

Commonly, such images are controlled by a strong professional ethic and laws defining the public use and distribution of forensic and medical data. Furthermore, other regulative orders related to public morality were raised to avoid any possible desecration of the privacy of the deceased person, not being able to self-defend any more against an action performed against them, as they have now become mere objects.[266]

Transgression of traditional Western morality and related social habits with regard to death, such as ceremonies, norms and rules of farewells traditions, condolences and mourning, were surely enforced by contemporary media trivializations of death. Photographs in media reports are the dominant broadcasters of discourse of death, they commonly hide identifiers of the deceased, to avoid possible charges of necrophilia, though they can still be blamed for desecration and utilization of dead.[267]

With the popularization of the CSI serials, fundamentally changing our relationship towards corpses, the barrier is broken, introducing vulgarly detailed dissection of bodies into our living rooms. And it continues further as pictures of death started proliferating along with other images. The number of pictures of the dead popping up on the internet is astonishing. Selfies with cadavers, breaking ethics of both forensics and medicine are haunting net society these days. Some authors, proudly publishing their selfies with dying or dead people, are leaving many immobilized by their senselessness, moral unscrupulousness and total corruption of respect owed to the dead.

Washington Times, 10 December 2013, http://www.washingtontimes.com/news/2013/dec/10/obama-takes-selfie-mandelas-funeral-service/.

265 Concept used by Jonathan Sawday, *The Body Emblazoned: Dissection and the Human Body in Renaissance*, Florence: Taylor and Francis, 2013.

266 Names for dead bodies change in regard to the discourse. Most of images that are tagged as *dead bodies* online arrive from contemporary news reels, reporting on some conflict fatalities, using images of dead bodies to spectacularize their reports, and draw attention to the textual report. There are stock agencies offering staged images of seemingly dead bodies, meant to serve as illustrations. The medical concept of the cadaver is used to mark the dead body in medical institutions, as medical centers, hospitals, or different asylums appears. Cadavers represented, contrary to images of dead bodies may appear in advanced status of decay. Contrary to disguising medical imagery, querying for the topic of corpses gets images in the horror aesthetic style, besides movies being connected to Halloween and heavy metal musical bands.

267 Susan Sontag, *On Photography*, New York: Farrar, Strauss and Giroux, 1977.

But what is so scandalous about a selfie with a cadaver that was not so scandalous in Victorian death photography? What is so necrophiliac in an image with a corpse that was not already present, in photographing a funeral or dead children, in the photographic history of the 19th century?

General Theory of the Dead

Photography is all about death, many theorists have repeated.[268] Even when not recording corpses, but living people, photographs end up representing death for a mere material reason; photographic pictures are more durable than human lives, some existing for already more than hundred and seventy years, as zombies.

Reference to death in photographic theory is thus unavoidable. Almost as if it could be stated; it is photography which invented the death discourse in full, as previously there were only sporadic writings on the theme. To quickly remind you of these themes; Siegfried Kracauer was the first to recognize the relationship of photography to death, while Walter Benjamin elaborated further on the effect of mortuary in photography, recognizing the *rigor mortis,* the stiffness of body muscles appearing within the first hours since passing and lasting for four days, a long-lasting effect of photography.[269] Benjamin defined photographic practice as neither artistic, nor forensic.[270] André Bazin introduced a metaphor of the photograph as the death mask of reality to describe the whole effect of technology that was later elaborated by Susan Sontag in the idea of the mummified effect of the medium.[271] No matter whether the picture represents a living or a deceased person, all of them concluded that each and every picture appears to be representing a latent image of death. Or, as Barthes summed up; no matter if the body is dead or alive, according to photography it is almost necessarily dead.[272] Barthes also defined the medium of photography *via* the concept of the memory of the moment that has already passed [Lat. *memento mori*]. Memento mori still was not the dying moment of the person, but the moment in which the person is found missing after its presentation in the photograph, so the photograph represented a certain love for death, a fascination with it. Barthes continued; 'Ultimately, what I am seeking in the photograph taken of me […] is Death: Death is the *eidos* of that Photograph.'[273]

Although not referring to selfies with cadavers at the time of writing, nor direct representation of death in photography, Barthes introduced the topic of general metaphorical deadness in photography, describing a very contemporary shift of the representation of death, nowadays centered around the narrator; the 'I' of the photograph, not the other object of his own record.

268 Barthes, *Camera Lucida*; Hans Belting, *An Anthropology of Images: Picture, Medium, Body*, Princeton and Oxford: Princeton University Press, 2011, being the most focused on the topic of deadness of photography.

269 Siegfried Kracauer, *Theory of Film: The Redemption of Physical Reality*, New Jersey: Princeton University Press, 1997; Walter Benjamin, 'A Short History of Photography' in Allan Trachtenberg (ed.) *Classic essays on photography*, New Haven: Leete's Island Books, 1980 (1931): 199-216.

270 Benjamin, *A Short History of Photography*.

271 André Bazin, 'The Ontology of Photographic Image', *Film Quaterly* 13.4 (1960): 4-9. Sontag, *On Photography*.

272 Barthes, *Camera Lucida*.

273 Barthes, *Camera Lucida*, p. 16.

Necrophilia and Necrophobia

While photographic discourse often refers to death, the topic of death is very rare in the general field of cultural theory till the 80s. Contemporary theory, especially French authors, like Maurice Blanchot or Jacques Derrida, but mostly Julia Kristeva, broke down the anxiety towards negative concepts of death in general.[274] By suggesting that the whole discourse around death was contaminating, Kristeva provided us with a reason why death as a topic was avoided. Death is something we have to get rid of, before it starts decaying in front of our eyes. She writes;

> A decaying body, lifeless, completely turned into dejection, blurred between the inanimate and the inorganic, a transitional swarming, inseparable lining of a human nature whose life is indistinguishable from the symbolic – the corpse represents fundamental pollution. A body without soul, a non-body, disquieting matter, it is to be excluded from God's territory as it is from his speech.[275]

Kristeva continues, 'The corpse, seen without God and outside of science, is the utmost of abjection. It is death infecting life.'[276] Dead bodies should not be touched, as they are impure and infect life. The only purification is the symbolic ceremony of the funeral. But why then should someone photograph the dead body? According to Kristeva's distinction, this is done by perverts, as there are: 'Corpse fanciers, unconscious worshippers of a soulless body, are thus preeminent representatives of inimical religions, identified by their murderous cults.'[277]

In Absence and in Presence (Cultural Necrophilia and Cultural Necrophobia)

So, besides death in photography there are photographs of death. Death in photography appears on a real and symbolic level, through presence and absence of life or person. One may also speak of the presence and absence of death; death in absence presents an image lacking a dead body, for example the image of the sarcophagus, while a death in presence displays the dead body itself, for example a corpse.

Images of death in presence and death in absence present a great deal of our visual culture today. Photographs reporting a person as being alive, meaning in absence, are commonly employed for memorial purposes, while photographs of the last moments looking like a human, or death in presence, are commonly used by mass media. Absences and presences of death may present a higher rank of the cultural production than the production of the individual image.

274 Maurice Blanchot and Jacques Derrida, *The Instant of my death. Demeure: Fiction and Testimony,* trans. Elizabeth Rottenberg, Meridian Crossing Aesthetics series, Redwood City: Stanford University Press, 2000; Jacques Derrida, *The Gift of Death,* trans. David Wills, Second Edition & Literature in Secret (Religion and Postmodernism), Chicago and London: University of Chicago Press, 1996 (1992); Kristeva, *Powers of Horror.*

275 Kristeva, *Powers of Horror,* p. 109.

276 Kristeva, *Powers of Horror,* p 4.

277 Kristeva, *Powers of Horror,* p. 109.

These two practices can be slightly exaggerated, to reintroduce the concept of Kristeva recognized on a cultural rather than a psycho-pathological level; necrophilia, and adding to it necrophilia's logical counterpart; necrophobia. Cultural necrophilia can be recognized in any mechanically and physically continuous representation of a dead body, a corpse, via photographic equipment, being the prosthesis of sight, but also on the symbolic level when depicting any person or even an alive one, in the context-discourse of the deadness itself.[278] Cultural necrophobia, to the contrary, can be seen in any of the occasions when the image fails, for any reason, to represent the corpse. As obvious, both concepts frame the same phenomena of a person's death, but one sets it out as a vulgar representation, while the other seeks a rather complex rhetoric, which can still easily fall into a kitsch aesthetics of 20th century representations of death.

Visualizing Death

The symbolic representation of death was preferred throughout the whole history of civilization, leaving the presentation of the corpse rare and strictly controlled.[279] In the visual arts, death was commonly represented on a necrophobic, or symbolic level, as for example in an allegory of death represented as a skeleton in a dark robe, dancing its dance of death [Fr. *danse macabre*]. Besides graphic representations, as for example Hans Holbein's *Danse Macabre* (1538), being maybe the most famous in the genre, there are a few pictures representing the actual corpse in art history.[280] One of the most interesting depictions of the cadaver is *The Anatomy Lesson of Dr. Nicolaes Tulp*, by Rembrandt van Rijn (1632). *The Anatomy Lesson* depicts a yearly public dissection, organized by the Amsterdam Guild of Surgeons.[281] This picture was painted in times characterised by the end of the Catholic idea that only the intact body will resurrect, raising what Jonathan Sawday named a 'culture of dissection'.[282]

At the beginning, mimicking the paintings of the era, even the technology of photography exercised both symbolic and real representations of death. Soon, after the official presentation of the invention of the medium to the French Academy of Science, death was staged in the photographic settlement or *mise-en-scène*. As already mentioned, photography by French photographer Bayard connoted in the message written on the back of the photograph that it was Daguerre who had robbed his invention. The picture depicted Bayard *laying as-if-dead* in front of his own camera.

With the popularization of the medium, the practice of recording death spread. The first practice was recorded only two years after the invention of photography.[283] Isaac A. Wetherby

---

278 And relate it to my previous works. See: Ana Peraica, *Victims Symptom: PTSD and Culture*, Amsterdam: Institute of Network Cultures, 2009.
279 Sarah Webster Goodwin and Elizabeth Bronfen, *Death and Representation*, *(Parallax: Re-visions of Culture and Society Series)*, Baltimore: Johns Hopkins University Press, 1993.
280 Among others were illustrations as ones for Andreas Vesalius', *De humani corporis fabrica*, (1543).
281 The corpse presented belonged to the criminal Aris Kindt (alias of Adriaan Adriaanszoon) while all doctors presented actually paid to be represented on this group portrait. The event itself was real, still the scene was staged.
282 Jonathan Sawday, *The Body Emblazoned: Dissection and the Human Body in Renaissance*, Florence: Taylor and Francis, 2013. Only about mid 15th century dissection was allowed by Pope Sixtus IV. See also: Klaver, *Sites of Autopsy in Contemporary Culture*.
283 Hillel Schwartz, *Culture of the Copy: Striking Likenesses, Unreasonable Facsimiles*, New York: Zone Books, 1996.

used daguerreotypes to record corpses in the mortuary, so he could paint their portraits after death [Lat. *post-mortem*].[284] This practice seemed so common that it was mentioned by Benjamin as well.[285] Benjamin wrote down that mortuary photography co-existed with other photographic genres 'since ever' for no particular reason, or as he wrote 'hardly anyone could know the reason why,' apart from the fact that 'everyone is doing that'.[286]

Reason for the expansion of the genre, seen from today's perspective, can be connected to the limits of technology. Early photography needed a longer exposure, sometimes up to fifteen or even twenty minutes, as in the case of Nadar's recording of the Paris sewer system, so corpses were more often preferred to be models than humans, as they would be incapable of sitting still. Furthermore, photography enhanced the possibility of research from a distance for newborn disciplines such as forensics, now enhanced to record and analyze the corpse out of the range of its specific smell of decay.

Still, the capacity of photography was far from the one of painting that is visible in Robinson's photograph entitled *Lady of Shalott* (1861), which has, for example, the same visual motif as the painting *Ophelia* (1851-2) by pre-raphaelite Millais. In both paintings, a woman floats dead on the river, but while the painting seems realistic, the photograph had hardly any capacity of representing such a scene in a realistic manner.

By the 1830s, posing dead became the genre of the epoch, Romanticism, consequently ending in the photographic movement of Pictorialism, besides staging allegoric deaths of heroines, also influenced popular aesthetics that saw death as immortal, beautiful, *sans* the errors and imperfections of existence. Still, the results of paintings and photographs with the same motifs were hardly comparable at the time.

The practice of photographing death reached its peak in the Victorian age. Images commonly featured corpses of deceased children for the reason they never succeeded in getting photographed alive.[287] Victorian representations of death and corpses were meant to rather necrophiliacally depict the deceased. However, the corpses were not presented as dead, they were staged as if being alive. Still, in Victorian portraits with the dead, it is quite impossible to grasp if the person is indeed dead, acting as dead or sleeping, as they were set against natural environments, supported by chairs or spine holders.[288] Sometimes, they are staged as if asleep. Occasionally, they are dressed in black clothes, lying immobile on the desk, as a piece of meat to be prepared. And very rarely there are coffins, decorated with flowers and candles. Even without them, sometimes, it is possible to recognize death by the surrounding atmosphere; the reactions of others, people assisting the dead, at the same time revealing sadness and disgust. If one looks more carefully, then one can detect the stiffness of the body, eyes half-closed, the gaze unfocused and lips unconcealed, but these occasions are rare. Such Victorian staged photographs served as evidence of life after death, the meeting of two parallel universes of the living and the dead.

---

284 Benjamin, *A Short History of Photography.*
285 Benjamin, *A Short History of Photography.*
286 Benjamin, *A Short History of Photography.*
287 Peters, in this Victorian fascination with death sees the opposition to contemporary society fascinated with sex which Victorian culture tabooed. Peters, *Speaking Into the Air.*
288 Visual culture often presented alive beings as the very carriers of death, in the less concrete, rather symbolic, metaphorical and allegoric manner. In many cases, still, it is impossible to figure out if the body photographically represented is indeed dead or alive, as has, for example shown a large debate on Capa's Falling Soldier (1936).

Besides, in arranging corpses, staging *tableaux vivants*, Victorians also engaged in shooting funerals and ghosts.[289] Contrary to deceiving double exposures, serving to prove the co-presence of ghosts, funeral photographs are recorded even to this day. Photographs of funerals can be a good anthropological resource, showing different cultural relationships to death, as well as practices around it. Such is the case, for example, of the photograph of an Afro-American funeral taken by James Van Der Zee, dated 1933, where an Afro-American lady is recorded in the coffin, surrounded by flowers.[290] The amount of flowers seems to be describing a completely different social stratum than the one a deceased belonged to. While the death itself is not staged, everything surrounding it is.

289 Photographs of ghosts were produced by double exposure of the negative. The first time such a
     phantasm probably occurred by accident, as a consequence of reusing badly washed glass negatives.
     It was Campbell's 'ghost photograph', dating back to 1860, that was the first one publicly disposed.
     Presented to the American Photographic Society it provoked a large public debate. According
     the author's statement, an image of a boy on the chair, whom he didn't know or has previously
     photographed, suddenly appeared in front of him. William Murnier, one of the most famous Victorian
     photographers of ghosts, went even further by testing public naivety, claiming he has seen and
     recorded spirits of Lincoln, Beethoven and many other historical figures, he himself has never met
     in real, but who now are visiting his own atelier. Murnier was, in consequence, publicly accused for
     deceiving his customers into believing they could communicate not only to dead members of the family
     but also ones they have never met.
     This bizarre practice of using photography for proving the existence of non-physical entities, reached
     its peak under extravagant theories challenging Darwinism itself. One of them, Transcendentalism,
     formulated by the 'medium' Margaret and Katie Fox had a goal of recording changes of *ectoplasm* on
     the occasion of one's death. Its USA variant, Mesmerism, had impacts on experiments with so called
     'second reality', being paralleled by philosophy of Idealism in Europe, according to Adorno.
290 James Van Der Zee was recording funerals 1930-60, images were latter reassembled on the internet.
     See for example: 'Death in Harlem', *CNN*, 25 April 2014, http://edition.cnn.com/2014/04/24/living/
     gallery/vanderzee-death/index.html.

Looking Death in the Mirror

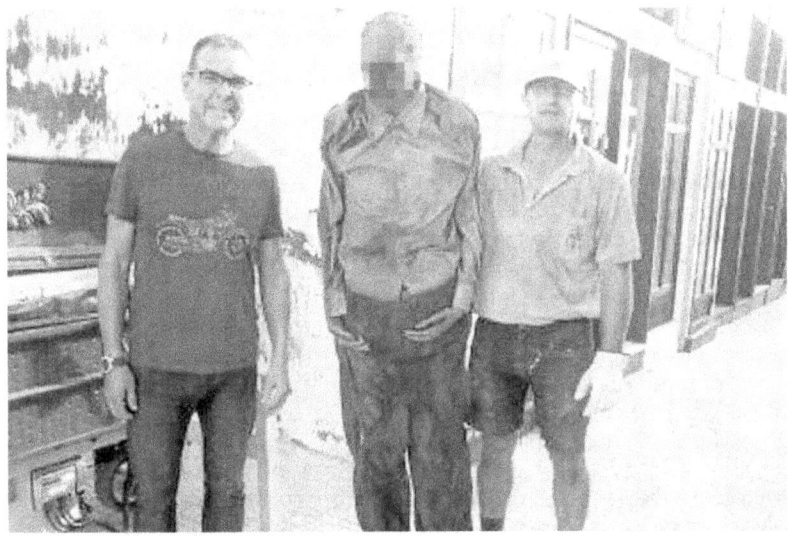

Image 11 – Selfie with exhumed cadaver (2014).

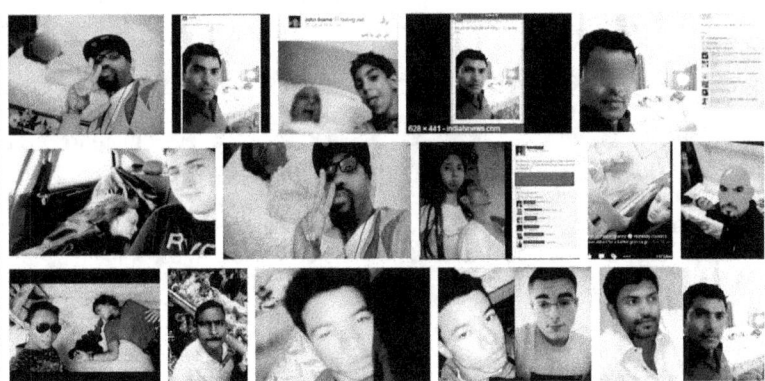

Image 12 – Selfies with deceased persons (Google search, 2016).

Contrary to Victorian representations of the dead, in which it is hard to decide if the person is dead or alive, contemporary selfies enlarge the difference at both real and symbolic levels.

The Victorian age has developed and elaborated the *poïesis* of mourning, in which showing a close relationship to a person deceased, while contemporary selfies indicate a sadomasochistic relationship towards the body of the particular Other, the other not being able to self-defend. Bodies are deprived of respect and used unwillingly, thus in a sadist manner.[291] In most cases, there is hardly any inner relationship visible to the body in the photograph, and the relationship to corpses in selfies with cadavers remains impersonal, devoid of physical touch or emotional reactions.

I took four images for analysis; in two out of four images, I have even found two authors laughing like psychopaths. In the third one, a subject refers to a dead body as an object with a deathly cold expression. Finally, in one a person shows emotions, a guy driving a car with a dead person is crying. Because of the arrangement of the image, in which the dead person appears in the second plane of the image, I cannot even assume the relationship of the author towards the person deceased. But, despite this lack, recording from the back can show, if not a relationship to the dead person, then a relationship to death.

This turning of one's back to death seems like a performance of courage, produced by pure fear. Similarly, sadistic laughter at the dead person that cannot react resonates with the hysterical panic reaction to the event of death. In all pictures, apart from the one in which a man is crying, there is a considerable distance between the people self-portraying and the corpses. The distance magnifies a psycho-pathological atmosphere of fears suppressed and denied, producing a surreal atmosphere. By turning their back to death, paradoxically enough, they show their own necrophobia, while at the same time necrophiliacally recording it.

A dead body is desecrated, and it cannot fight back. Corpses cannot get hurt, will not get offended, so all the human actions will mean nothing to them. It is we, the audience, that are hurt and terrified, as we are faced with a sadistic author, pushing us to the scene of death to which s/he turns his own back, as once Caravaggio's Narcissus has kicked us out of the scene. It is we who are being placed in an abject position that we must defend by means of laughter. Thus, the image functions on the metonymic level, interchanging a sense of aggression between the person recording and the public, not the person recorded.

Speaking in terms of the *mise-en-scene* of a directed scene, or even more the actual scenography in which a dead body is used, the selfie of a woman laughing in front of a coffin becomes interesting. In a hospital selfie, where a person is self-recorded in the forensic laboratory, the body is placed in the distance, to the left side of the image. In funeral selfies, the distance among plans is about two or more meters. Although most of the mobile phones use wide lenses, both the author and the corpse are similarly sharpened, visually appearing farther than in reality.

But, if one reads the symbolic perspective, the cadaver is usually placed on the shoulder of the author. It functions as a symbolic threat, no matter which relationship the author aims to establish by his/her own scrupulous smile, appearing in a similar place like the one rationalist Perseus has positioned the real Medusa in, so to be able to control her and master reality, almost like a scientist.

---

291 Dita Pepe, Tomoko Sawada, Petra Mrša, Trish Morrissey et al.

The position of the corpse in the back, at the place of the vanishing point, can be related to the metaphysical reading of a vanishing point, in James Elkins and Friedrich Kittler.[292] Elkins describes the modern approach to perspective as Saturnian, melancholic.[293] Kittler, on the other hand, described the pyramidal structure of perspective always necessarily ending with an absence, or non-place. All perspective paintings are placed around a hole, he claimed.[294]

At the same time, while the vanishing point in which the object is set exists, the space of the audience and the space of the author changes. First, the intended public of the Victorian death photography is not the same as the one of selfies; Victorian selfies were made for a specific private purpose while selfies with cadavers go viral.[295] Thus, a dead person in an image is an empty signifier, while there is a personal relationship between the audience and the Victorian images of death.

Reality Pushed Behind One's Back

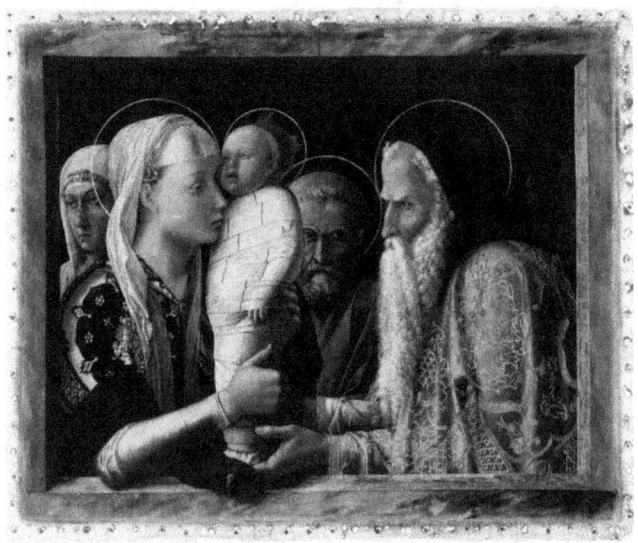

Image 13 – Mantegna erased from the Presentation at the Temple (1455).

---

292 Elkins, *The Poetics of Perspective*. See also: Friedrich A. Kittler, *Perspective and the Book,* trans. Sara Ogger *Grey Room* 5 (2001).
293 'The possibilities of speaking about perspective in the language of loss and mourning are typically modern.'; Elkins, *The Poetics of Perspective*, p. 4.
294 Elkins, *The Poetics of Perspective*, p. 4.
295 Bal in the interpretation of the caricature Arjuna's Penance, distinguishes the object, the subject, the focalizer and the focalizing object. See: Bal, *Looking in: The Art of Viewing*, p. 50. It is possible to extract the narrative of the selfie with cadavers, using those terms; the image contains a fable telling, a person has died and was recorded by someone, who directly addresses me, but not the deceased person. Still, the story seems to be told by the dead person observing from the back.

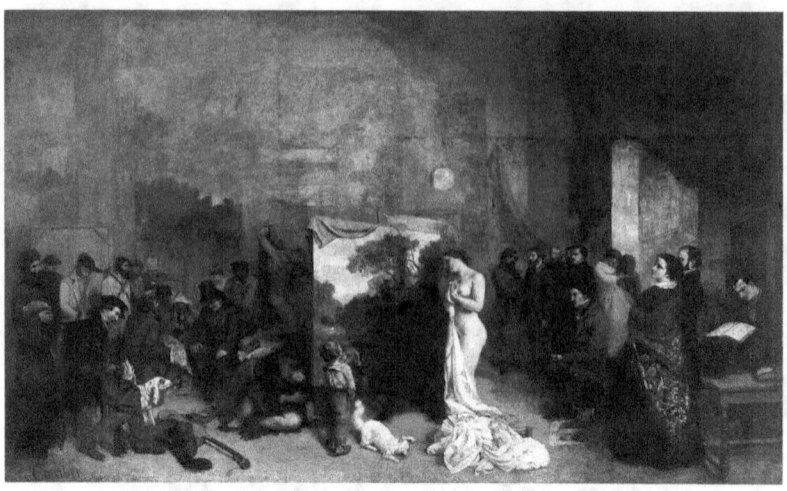

Image 14 – Courbet erased from his The Painter's Atelier (1855).

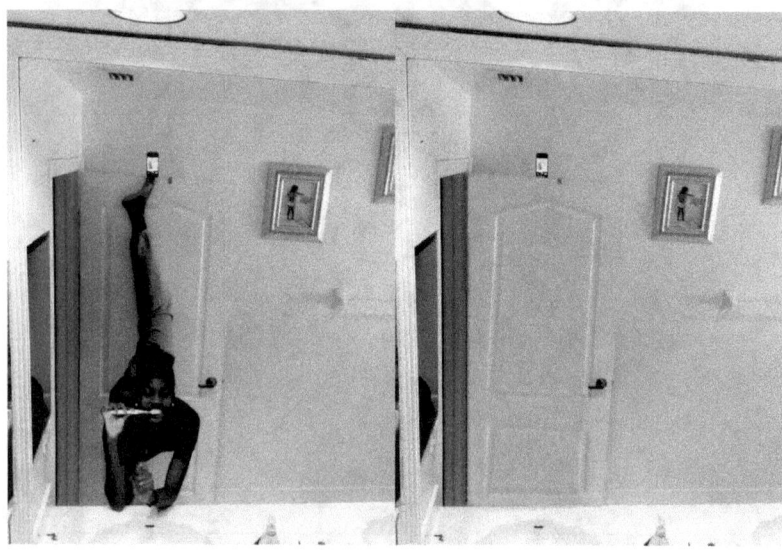

Image 15 – Selfie with person erased.

The relationship to self and reality pushed at the back, can be illustrated by another ancient myth referring to the use of mirrors, not for a tragedy of self-love as in Narcissus, but mastering of the reality, in the myth of Perseus.[296] Perseus had a task; to behead a Gorgon Medusa.[297] He used the reflection in the polished shield, provided by Athena, in order to weaken Medusa's ability to turn people into stone if they looked at her.

Paradigmatic antagonism of the myths of Narcissus and Perseus, already recognized by Simon Blackburn, also lies in the perception of external reality, and its reflection.[298] In the case of Narcissus, the reflection is the same as the perceiver, who is also the object. In the case of Perseus, the reflection is of someone else, from whom the perceiver is radically divided by the reflection. While Narcissus lives in a self-sufficient universe, based on a self-approving tautology, Perseus uses the same reflection to observe and control outside reality, in which a dangerous being is hunting. Whereas Narcissus is self-sufficient, Perseus on the other hand is not. He is dependent on the outside reality, forming indirect, critical, and rational relationships with it. Even more, Perseus uses the reflection for knowing. While Narcissus fails to know, Perseus becomes the hero – egoist, according to Simon Blackburn, defining one as a paradigm of irrationality, while the other one of rationalism based on planning.[299] While for Narcissus, Echo is the measure, for Perseus it is himself. So, the difference between the two mythical paradigms underlines the different order between subjects, objects and viewers in reality, as well a relationship towards reality. While Echo observes Narcissus, who falls into illusion, it is Perseus who controls reality without assistance. Still, his reality is not set in front of him, rather – behind his back.

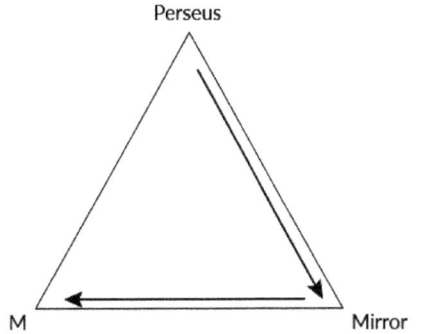
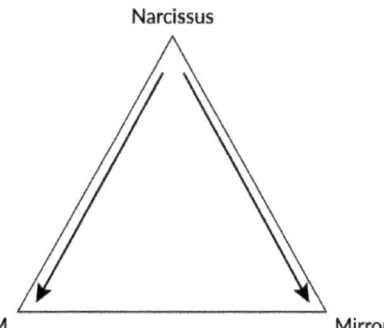

Graph 4 – The way reflection brings cognition in myth of Perseus and Narcissus: Perseus cannot see reality (M) directly but only via mirror; while Narcissus sees directly and simultaneously self and reality in which self appears.

296 Simon Blackburn, *Mirror, Mirror: The Uses and Abuses of Self Love*, Princeton and Oxford: Princeton University Press, 2014.
297 Ovid, Metamorphoses, IV: 792-802.
298 Blackburn, *Mirror, Mirror.*
299 The difference between the narcissist and egoist is, according to Blackburn, egoist as he 'achieves self-knowledge, but cannot use it'. Blackburn, *Mirror, Mirror*, p. 39.

Hiding behind the camera, in a world of visual imaging, rather than reality that world photographers of images of death see and construct, is at the same time mediated and non-mediated, as they are different to every eye. It is mediated in terms of being set closer, for the parts of the message going through the channel. Simultaneously, other parts of the world are muted, as set into a distance bridged by lenses. As inputs are twisted, so the photographer, at least on a sensory level, does not have a full feeling of 'being into' the world. He is cognitively excluded from a world of occasions, being concentrated on a future image of it. Namely, he is engaged in directing a completely different, world of future memories on the occasion recorded. He has to make choices in amplifying his own narration by camera angles, providing engagement with the choice of lenses and focus, producing atmosphere and symbolism with the depth of the field. Thus; not only he is not physically there, but also there is nothing more in the image than the fact that he is only being there.[300]

Once he has put himself inside a scene, he jumps into a cruel reality and the photographer assumes his responsibility for participation, becoming discursively mortal.[301] Defining oneself as a mortal person, but also alive person that can memorize, he is also willingly allowing himself to get traumatized. He becomes only one of us, a mortal being, having nothing to do with the eternally vampiric nature of photography. Each photographic self-portrait is necessary for a descent of the author into reality, and images with the dead show this in a full capacity. So, that is how the selfie with cadavers functions in regard to the indirect experience of reality, in which the author is sinking too.

300 As I have elaborated in my thesis. See: Ana Peraica. *Fotografija kao dokaz.*
301 Susan Sontag, *Regarding the pain of others*, New York: Picador, Farrar Strauss and Giroux, 2003.

VI. TECHNOLOGY OF RECORDING

Mirrors are described in terms of portraits and portraits in terms of mirrors.[302]

Technological Emancipation

To approach the interaction between the perceiving subjects and perceived subjects-as-objects of self-portraiture, it is crucial to understand changes introduced by technology's development. Technological emancipation of masses, meaning their slow overtaking of technologies, has brought numerous novelties to the world of self-imaging, depicting individualism which was commonly strongly contrasted to the image of the mass.

It took about a century to calibrate self-imaging technologies. The first revolution occurred with the invention of the ready-made 35mm film, succeeding the invention of the portable Brownie Kodak camera, followed by a series of inventions of gadgets and tools such as; self-timers, exposure meters, all leading to the fully automatic camera, colloquially named the 'idiot' in succeeding years.[303] The process was finally completed with the invention of rewritable media. New possibilities of recording enhanced something, for which nearly two hundred years of photographic history needed to have someone else doing it – a photographer, whose profession is now disappearing altogether with his medium, into everyone's hobby.[304]

Apart from the photographer, the subject and the interpreter have changed too. With changes in photographic technologies stabilizing our image into the picture, inescapably the view on the self is transformed. Today's (self) portraits are, due to technological limits, but also fall of visual criteria introduced by professionals, slowly being accepted as red-eyed, concaved, and pixilated, completely different than presentations of humans at the beginning of photographic history. Moreover, the image has become genuine, mass-like, failing to depict the individual self-portrayed, for mere technological reasons, as I will show.

Light Limits

When a strong light-source is too near, the record of the face can turn, if recorded by automatic image technologies, as overexposed and flat. Without shadows that plastically describe individual features in detail, the photography ceases to be itself, a three-dimensional illusion made in two dimensions.

Photographic space is defined not as empty space but as a medium, a light carrier that can be emphasized by additional light sourcing. Light has been used, through the history of the development of photography to detach a person from his surroundings. By introducing three-dimensional illusion into two-dimensional media, light indicates the existence of space

---

302 Sabine Melchior-Bonnet, *The Mirror: A history*, p. 152.
303 Brownie was invented by Kodak in 1901, one of earlier self-timers was invented in 1902, first automatic exposure was developed 1983, also by Kodak.
304 On the disappearance of photography, Flusser writes; 'Photography is about to become redundant.' Vilem Flusser, *Into the universe of technical images*, p. 45.

between subjects and objects, objects and backgrounds, backgrounds and spaces and so forth, to be able to define or describe them. With the disappearance of the background light, the space in which objects appear is now becoming rather a subjective space, showing no other or outer space of existence than the one between the person and the camera. On the other hand, where the light grows in the back – the world behind the back of the author of the selfie becomes more important.

Besides, light in photographic portrait is used for deeper psychologization, which comes as inter-individual interpretation. If there is anything a photographic medium, as a medium of continuous physical reality, of light, cannot represent it is inner physiological activity and the psychological condition of the subject. But they can be mimicked by so called 'psychological lighting' on a technical level, adding to a common list of psychologization effects in visual culture, such as; posing, context, or text.

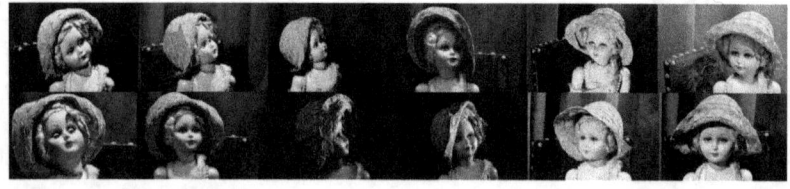

Image 16 – Light changes 'character' – test of light on a doll (2011, my photo).

Contrary to classic portrait technologies, the mobile phone hardly has any possibility of lighting space descriptions and psychologization that a studio portrait has (even if there are external flashes built for mobile phones too, they are rarely used). Because of a different space description, flash-beam of a mobile phone and a modeling studio light are substantially different. While for a regular studio portrait there are, at least, three strobes; with the selfie there is only a single light supply, usually incorporated within the camera itself. Direct flash into the face, with inbuilt flashes, makes most selfies unidentifiable in terms of individual face characteristics and features. All the losses in lighting of the portrait are automatically refunded by slowing the shutter speed and raising the ISO settings. In consequence, high sensitivity disintegrates the picture into elementary pixels, visible in most of the selfies seen on larger screens of monitors, producing an aura wherever the light touches a contour of an object in the counter-light. Alternatively, when there is not enough light to record the digital camera automatically raises the sensitivity-pushing camera to depict real lighting in yellowish gamma, so that the skin gains an unnatural smoker's color.

Wide and Telephoto Lenses

The face of contemporary Narcissus, besides being pale, is very often distorted because of the camera lens. While classic portrait photography records people with mild telephoto lenses, mobile phone technology usually uses fixed wide lenses.[305] Wide lenses can depict the scene that is sharp at almost all points, while telephoto lenses produce distances between areas defined sharply and areas out of the sharpness zone.[306] The second reason why telephoto lenses are used is to avoid space deformation, present with wide lenses. Besides the subject's features, wide-lens technology also provides distorted space description, much more of the space is visible than it is by the human eye in general and the space is described from a closer point. The crop out of reality changes with wide lenses.[307] Namely, the human eye does not see so close and so wide, without a turning of the head.[308] Shooting a portrait with a wide lens may produce distribution of the facial elements appearing deformed similar to the self-image that one sees reflected in a spoon.

Portrait and Snapshot Mode

Selfies are recorded rather in a snapshot than a portrait mode. As mobile technology generally has a deficiency of light for its construction, it is hard to record in a slow mode. Contrary to selfies, timing of recording a classic portrait is slowed down, conditioned by a slowness of the equipment itself. Arthur Danto suggested, in analysis of classic portraits, that there is an intrinsic relationship of the portrait with the technique of slow exposure.[309] No matter the sensitivity of the film or camera's chip, no matter the light capacity of the lens, to portray, he noted, means to record in a slow mode, below the 60th part of a second.[310] While to portray is to slow down, to snapshot is to speed up. De Duve has described the abyss between two types of photography even more radically, commenting; 'We have discovered the manic-depressive functioning of the photograph by insisting on the didactic opposition of snapshot and time exposure.'[311]

Snapshot photography, like selfies, belong to a street photography genre, exactly for the difference between posing and movement, staging and catching, introducing certain deadness in the discourse of a studio portrait. Another difference between the portrait and snapshot mode is that for a portrait there are few images recorded, while for snapshot photography catching unique moments, there are commonly dozens. A portrait photographer has to take more photographs until the subject relaxes, while reportage photography takes even more shots in order to sequence the movement.

---

305 Ranging from 80mm to 120mm.

306 Many of early photography portraits were not sharp, and some authors implemented an unfocused image as a style, as for example Margaret Cameron. Her soft focus was laying out as a filter of unreality, melting face lines into an un-sharp a non-contrasted image, without specific facial shadows or wrinkles. Jonathan Crary, *Techniques of the Observer*, p. 2.

307 The mirror, as for example, provides close and far full focus in its reflexivity, while optical equipment has to focalize sharp on a particular distance, depending on the construction of lenses.

308 Binocular vision is 200 degrees in total. See: Hershenson, *Visual Space Perception*.

309 Arthur C. Danto, 'The Naked Truth', in Scott Walden (ed) *Photography and Philosophy: Essays on the Pencil of Nature*, New Jersey: Blackwell Publishing, 2008, 284-309.

310 Danto, *The Naked Truth*.

311 Thierry de Duve, 'Time Exposure and Snapshot: The Photograph as Paradox', *October* 5 (Summer, 1978): 113-125.

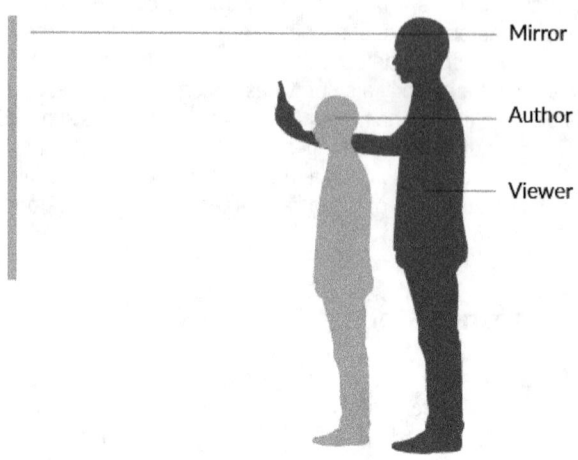

Graph 5 – Spacing differences between portrait, self-portrait and selfie.

Number of Shots in a Serial Sequence

Selfie photography appears as an amalgam of both being a portrait genre and recording number of pictures as in snapshot photography. Or, to put it in another way, behind every successful selfie there are a number of erased or not-uploaded similar pictures, not matching the idealized self-image.

Producing redundant imagery has become possible only since recently. The largest difference between chemo-mechanical processes of glass and film with digital process is related to the expense of the media that limits the number of shots. While the glass plates were exposed separately, one by one, film allowed multiple, but quite expensive exposures in a row. At the beginning these serials consisted of only few pictures in a sequence, because of the film's price. Digital revolution introduced re-writing carriers, for which the number of shots increased, introducing visual waste into the world.

Compared to the times when my grandfather made his own portrait, photographic equipment has become much easier to handle. My grandfather had to prepare negative glass plates on his own as there were hardly any ready-made negative plates on the market. After recording, because of numerous errors, as small cracks in the glass, uneven layers of the chemical coating, but also the light which was not set to the needs of photographer as today, he had to retouch pictures for hours. Newer media is less complicated, with stable and predictable quality, visible even in the act of portraying.

Replicability

Replicability of photography and its distribution were the key technological challenges of photographic history. Without a system of copying, photography was merely a mirror image fixed to a surface. Daguerreotype, for example, was a unique non-replicable object as well as a mentioned first self-portrait of Bayard, made directly on a single positive. The first distribution became possible only with the creation of manufacturing prototype, i.e. negative, literally a safe or master-copy out of which new copies were generated.[312]

Copies, at early times of film-based production, were hardly identical, due to their manufacturing conditions, in a darkroom with bare hands. Nevertheless, Walter Benjamin warned about a general loss of aura in photographic image for its capacity to reproduce the artifact in a number of copies.[313] Long after, the number of copies produced out of each negative was relatively small, as photography was rather an expensive analogue process.[314] The production of photographs became cheaper only fifty years after Benjamin's essay on reproducibility, with so-called C-process industry, introducing machines that could print out hundreds of photographs within only a minute, decreasing the price per photo nearly to one cent.

Even then, when the copy became economical, the self-portrait was not a genre that was commonly printed in hundreds of copies, but rather few ones. The reason lays in the embarrassment an amateur photographer had to face in-between producing and seeing his own picture; meeting a photo-laboratory worker, commonly a professional photographer, who might have criticized them for doing the job wrongly. Films were handed to photo studios with an enormous shame of exposing one's secret passion to self-record, a sin of narcissism, an excess of – self-love.

Digital photography revolution, changed the relationship of the replica and the original, completely destroying the meaning of the first copy, or the prototype as well, but also the idea of originality, as different versions of files started appearing. It has also provided complete privacy for users whose photographs were not seen by photo laboratories, symbolically murdering the inter-mediator in the photographic process – the photographer.

Internet has also provided a new possibility for picture distribution without any costs, introducing yet another risk of privacy control endangering boundaries of the private and the public. Series become unpredictable, copies multiplied even on a single computer, but also other echoing data carriers such as hard discs, memory sticks, memory cards, CDs, and DVDs, uploaded to private online backup, but also other computers as attached in a web-mail, sent to someone else, or to public social networks. Leaking copies appear as active, propagandistic items, centered on a single purpose or a political direction, if directed by activists, or floating without any clear purpose, on the wind of online amusement, waiting to become victims of their own vague meaning.

312 Talbot, *Pencil of Nature.*
313 Benjamin, *The Work of Art in the Age of Mechanical Reproduction.*
314 The argument of the expenses of media is often not taken seriously into the account; nevertheless, price of media can frame complete visual history, as shown in a number of photographic retouches during the Stalin's era, but also a Socialist realism as a practice. See for example; Boris Groys, *Dream Factory Communism*, Berlin: Hatje Cantz Publishers, 2003.

New technologies of auto-replicability of quick copies, and social platforms of quick forwarding framed a public space as a space of danger in which publicity itself behaves virally, as if alive; a malignant disease attacking body integrity.[315] Mutated copies though appearing identically the same, still, started changing meanings, shifting messages to other coding systems, in an uncontrolled and not necessarily meaningful way. Contrary to the 'culture of the copy,' as defined by Schwartz, with the contemporary crisis of the copy, a new condition is reached, in which a copy is no more distinguishable from a completely different version, producing a tiredness of the form.[316]

Distribution

The largest difference between the intimate Bayard self-portrait, commemorative and personal Victorian photographs, as well as stylistic death aesthetics of the Modern, is first of all in media distribution. Bayard's self-portrait was produced in a single copy positive print, while selfies are distributed massively and accidentally, as there is no limit to production of digital copies. They potentially have an unlimited number of copies, with unpredictable distributive destiny. 'Potentially identical beings (sign-*objects*) produced in indefinite series' as defined by Baudrillard, have started mutating, turning into potentially different objects that are produced in identical manners and series.[317]

Distribution and digital photography seem closer to organic *meiosis* than classic stamping of the paper. The number of generated copies is unpredictable, the distribution system is unforeseeable and framed by an arbitrary decision or the accidental movement of the mouse; 'like', 'forward'. Some of these pictures are themselves recorded by accident, as if the photographer has sat on the mobile phone. Some are published by accident, for example what happened to poor Geraldo Rivera, who posted his half-naked body with the caption; '70s are the new 50s', publishing it publicly by accident.[318] Some pictures were released by angry ex-boyfriends or hackers from the neighborhood.[319]

Even when not accidentally disseminated, and differently than portraits in family albums distributed diachronically, selfies are distributed synchronically, meaning; it is impossible to forecast which member, or group of audience, will accept and forward them. Being viral yet behaving as integral, selfies are not capable of adapting to different contexts. They can completely twist or deny the idea or even the identity of the author. As end users of a selfie are unknown and unforeseeable, so are its reactions. Hence selfies are basically unstable.

---

315 While on the other hand, it is precisely the public space that is disappearing in front of the private interest in the real world.

316 Schwartz, *Culture of the Copy*.

317 Jean Baudrillard, *Selected writings*, trans. Jacques Mourrain, Redwood City: Stanford University Press, 2002.

318 'I was drunk and lonely: Geraldo explains his half-naked selfie', *Page Six*, 23 July 2013, http://pagesix. com/2013/07/23/i-was-drunk-and-lonely-geraldo-explains-his-half-naked-selfie/.

319 There is a whole genre of so-called 'revenge porn', streamed at sites such as UgotPosted, IsAnyoneUp, etc.

Where too many self-portraits appear, none of them will become the most important one any more. Once they resemble each other is the moment they have become tiring, banal, representing a conventional or a generic self, the self that actually has no specificities or has confused them with something else.

Furthermore, selfies are ephemeral and non-important. Contrary to portraits and other self-portraits they are not broadcasting important events of someone's lives, as photography was, reporting for centuries, events such as birth, baptism, first day of school, weddings. And even if they do now, these events appear important as any other day. Selfies are unspecific, wide-ranging pictures. They report on arbitrary moments, which at the same time gain an important ontological place in our lives, appearing as subconscious and random stream of moments which meaning is absurdly amplified by their public exposure. There is something Dadaistic about this irrelevance, and also something Situationistic in these images produced by boredom.

Photographs were for hundreds of years glued into photographic albums, forming linear narratives, from event to event, or waiting in boxes for someone to sort them out. Whereas traditional photographic albums were not 'browsable' but read linearly; from one's birth to death, with succession based on events solely, selfie photographs appear in non-personalized online databases, hardly telling any story at all. This temporal arrangement represents a non-cinematic serial of self-obsessed consciousness that may end fatally.[320]

Not being organized in narrative order, but according to sets, the second characteristic of selfies is their redundancy with additional irrelevance. Websites on which they are uploaded are not fixed places, such as photo albums or photo archives of negatives once were, but are merely places where clouds temporarily gathered by the 'electricity' of connection make direct multi-wrapped references on social networks. The same network, mentioned by Crary long time ago, has grown since 1992, absorbing all private data, including the most private and intimate relationship to the self. In its last phase, of post-photography, subjectivity appears as not residing in the individual, but only in the network, behaving as if alive. And it is the same question raised by Crary that haunts the era of the uploaded self-portrait as it did the era of vision and the observer in two epochs, one of camera obscura, and one of photography, and that is: 'In what ways is subjectivity becoming a precarious condition of interface between rationalized systems of exchange and networks of information.'[321]

---

320 As for example in the case of selfie-obsessed teenager Danny Bowman taking approximately 200 photos a day, and finally becoming suicidal after not managing to make 'the perfect one'. See: Antonia Molloy, 'Danny Bowman Taking Approximately 200 Photos a day, and Finally Becoming Suicidal After not Managing to Make "The Perfect one"', The Independent, 24 March 2014, http://www.independent. co.uk/news/uk/home-news/selfie-obsession-made-teenager-danny-bowman-suicidal-9212421.html.

321 This question was raised by Crary, asking' 'How is the body, including the observing body, becoming a component of new machines, economies, apparatuses, whether social, libidinal or technological?' (...) In what ways is subjectivity becoming a precarious condition of interface between rationalized systems of exchange and networks of information?' Crary, Techniques of the Observer, p. 2.

VII. CONCLUSION

We don't know how to exist anymore without imaging ourselves as a picture.[322]

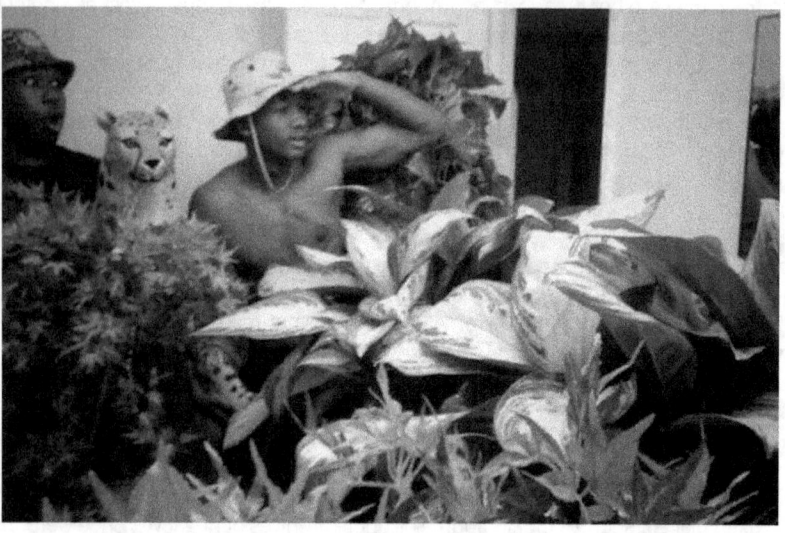

Image 17 – Selfie Olympics.

There are several strategies for producing self-portraits.[323] The first one is by directly looking and recording into the mirror, or using a shutter device. The second one is running into a staged scene, using the tripod or other means to fix the camera. The third works with the assistance of a third person who, at the same time, is not the author or a creator, but merely a button-presser.[324] Only the first strategy is the product of the direct and simultaneous gaze into the camera, and contains original processes of imaging and seeing, while the second and the third contain a postponed or trajectory gaze, that do not represent the original process of seeing oneself.[325] Staged images, moreover, introduce an epistemic confusion, where the

---

322 Melchior-Bonnet, *The Mirror*, p. XVII.
323 To make a painted self-portrait, one can use three different techniques: looking at oneself in a side positioned or straight positioned mirror; shooting 'on blind' with the assistance of a second person; imagining and reconstructing the scene, so called *tableaux vivants*. To make a photographic self-portrait, there are fewer options. A photograph can be taken in the mirror, as most of modern pre-shutter self-portraits are, which, if flashed with internal flash of the camera, may also erase – overexpose – the self-portrait. You can take a picture by hand, producing a crop of a shortened arm, or by timer-based *tableaux vivants* in which quite often the photographer finds himself in an unusual position, literary running into the scene. Only selfies with selfie-sticks make this process continuous; a person sees oneself while self-recording. They are simultaneous, providing an instant knowledge.
324 Fontcuberta sees two types of selfies. One of them is the mirror-selfie, *reflectogram,* having rhizomes in a long tradition of visual depiction of oneself in the mirror. While the other one presents an arm, usually called 'deictic arm', given by holding the camera in your hand. This is what Fontcuberta calls *autophoto.*
325 Derrida, *Memoirs of the Blind*.

author is catching up with time to replace the empty place, reserved for him in the scene imagined and constructed, so it would appear as he was recording himself retroactively, which he was not doing at all. Finally, when the second person records, there is a mediated sensorial experience of seeing through someone else's eyes, the eyes of the mirror, a memory of the scene, or through another person's eyes, forming a gaze. Or, as Derrida says, 'he does show himself, he does show up, but to the other.'[326]

As its name indicates, the mirror is connected to self-knowing.[327] Often it is connected to a meaning of 'mirror of introspection.' In his *Iconologia*, Cesare Ripa writes about the mirror as wisdom, prudence, truth, and personification of sight.[328] A similar idea has been employed by Dante's paradigm of the three mirrors of truth, and the mystics Saint Paul and Saint James who distinguish the deep gaze behind surfaces and surface gaze.[329] Another generalized idea of the glass representing the face of the world [Lat. *speculum mundi*], evoked in writings of Gottfried Wilhelm Leibniz, deploying the paradigm of mirroring, the reflection or picture made from the image of God.[330] 'Knowing thyself' with the use of mirror has always stayed a part of the mystical tradition.

The Mirror Itself

The selfie is a mirroring photograph, as the process of seeing is simultaneous to the one of recording, so the mirror often becomes the theme of the genre, evoking questions of knowing. One of the award-winning selfies during the first edition of The Selfie Olympics depicts a guy trapped in his own multiple reflections.[331] Shooting his selfie with a mobile phone and two notebooks, he produced the effect of a hall of mirrors, without actually using them. Such a play of mirrors was used for amusement in the Renaissance courts and 19th century mass fairs, and became a symbolic background for murder scenes in popular movie culture in the 20th century.

---

326 Derrida, *Memoirs of the Blind*, p. 12.

327 Ancient connections of knowing to looking are preserved in the Latin word for mirror, *speculum*, as well as the verb; meaning spying, watching, observing, examining, or exploring, in Latin *speculor*.

328 Cesare Ripa, *Iconologia, or, Moral Emblems* 1709, https://archive.org/details/iconologiaormora00ripa.

329 Evident in interpreting *speculatio* from *speculum*. Dante narrates a travel from *speculum inferius* to *superius* in the Divine Comedy.

330 Gottfried Wilhelm Leibniz, *The Principles of Philosophy known as Monadology*, 1714. http://www. earlymoderntexts.com/assets/pdfs/leibniz1714b.pdf. Similarly, it is expressed in the work of mystic and alchemist Joseph du Chesne. See: Joseph du Chesne, *Le Grand Miroir du Monde*, 1587, http://gallica. bnf.fr/ark:/12148/bpt6k5860952d.r=Le+grand+miroir+du+monde.langFR.

331 1st annual Selfie Olympics, 2014. Appearing in a selection of the magazine Wired. Jacob Schiller, '10 best selfies from Selfie Olympics', *Wired*, 1 October 2014, http://www.wired.com/2014/01/the-10-best-photos-from-the-selfie-olympics/.

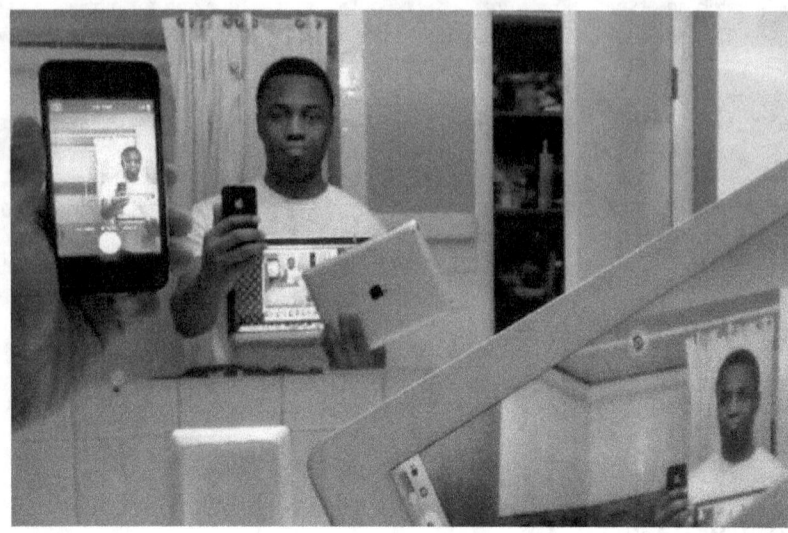

Image 18 – Selfie from Selfie Olympics (2014).

Mirrored reality introduces an ontological paradox in visual culture.[332] Different mirrored realities in this image are depending on the view angle, depicting diverse spatial constellations.
Because of the multiple images combined with each other, the room in this image appears
faceted, as seen in a broken glass, inscribing a proper cubist space. So, the mobile phone,
recording vertically, portrays a space of the shower half-covered with a curtain. The first
notebook, one positioned in the right hand, depicts the corner of the bathroom, uncovering
a part of the ceiling too. Then, the mirror that has the wide angle, lays out the whole space;
the shower, the guy, and a wardrobe with open doors of the closet to the left, but actually
positioned in the right side of the image. The second notebook, visible only in the mirrored
image, is hidden behind the scene, from where it inscribes the origin of the whole scene,
spreading all the imaging devices, including the mirror, having the widest view. The guy
recording appears to the right of this largest view. There are five converging space views; the
person into the mirror, the mirror into the person, the mobile into the mirror, the first laptop
into the mirror, and the second laptop into the mirror. Furthermore, each recorded image
consists of several sub-reflections; the reflection in the mirror, the same image recorded by
the mobile, the image recorded by one of the notebooks, the image recorded by the second
notebook, and then inside each of the recordings there is yet another fractal split of reality, multiplying the image endlessly. A single reality descends into a single reflection to be
captured by three devices and then reflected in loops, each new image progressing in the
mathematical operation of the square on fifth (n^5).

---

332 Also recognized by Lewis Carroll.

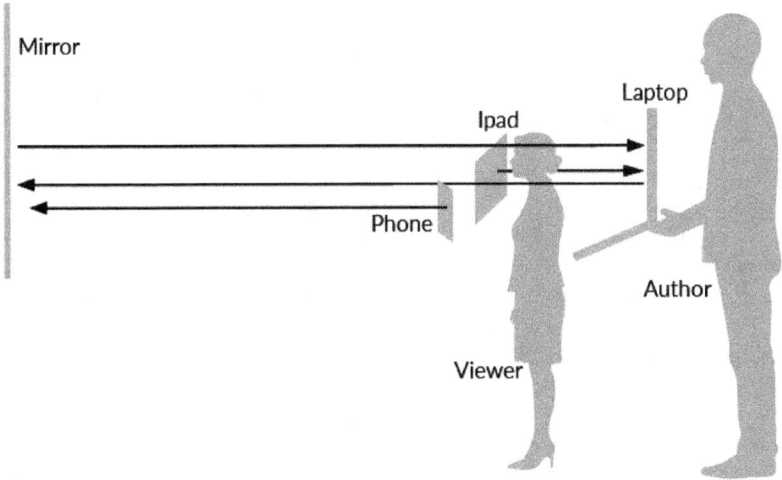

Graph 6 – Spacing in the selfie from Selfie Olympics, 2015. The different devices show the viewer another angle, so the space in front of the person recording is captured in a different way.

This space is additionally twisted from the side of the viewer, as the viewers are looking into the mirror not from the point of the person recording, as the viewpoint of the image is set lower. We see it from the viewpoint which is set at his lower abdomen as is the tablet, squeezed in-between his arms and his three gadgets. We are squeezed inside his immediate body space. Being situated lower, our angle is showing a less aesthetic part of the place, with basic ceramics and electric plug-in inside its mirrored reflection.

But the image also twists from the position of the viewer. Positioning the viewer, who has the widest picture on the described reality, very low as at the place of his own abdomen, the person recording the selfie also fails to see himself clearly in the self-portrait. Namely, his gaze into the mirror is higher than the viewpoint of the tablet that conditions the view of the viewer. Despite in the mirror they are continuous, seeing and recording do not appear as parallel processes, although they are simultaneous, and it is only us who see through the camera seeing.[333]

The space mirrored and recorded, and the space of mirroring and viewing overlap, but they are not the same. The place of our meeting is a bathroom, framed by a plastic white sheet of a standing shower on one side, with a built-in shelf to the other. It is a very simple bathroom, covered with cheap white ceramics, decorated with a frameless mirror glued directly onto the wall. The average appearance of the place is of a messy and tiny closet. It may be the private bathroom of the guy recording; a black guy in a simple white T-shirt. Then we are squeezed not only in the private view of the lower abdomen, but also in his intimate space.

---

333 To paraphrase Warburton. See: Nigel Warburton, 'Seeing Through "Seeing through photographs"', *Ratio* 1.1 (1988), DOI: 10.1111/j.1467-9329.1988.tb00111.

Mirrored Image

Between two images, mirrored and mirroring, motifs of self-portraiture seem to vanish. Why are we squeezed into the toilet? What is this simple guy, in his simple white T-shirt, with a modest bathroom doing with an iMac and iPhone, each in his own hands and even one pressed against his abdomen? Has he just unpacked new items, has he stolen them, has he won them in a lottery? Was this his dream, a goal achieved? Does he have someone in particular he wants to address his self-image to? And although I can imagine all the possible scenarios – he has robbed a shop, he has bought gifts for his girlfriend, has won a lottery and bought what he has dreamt of – the real message stays impenetrable to the public. Besides in context of self-representations in general, of ordinary people, this image from The Selfie Olympics can be decoded at the level of motifs, compared to the production of art historical sources, pregnant with self-images implementing mirrors and various imaging technologies.

Some of these images, using mirrors and technologies, show twists of mirrored reality. Others produce impossible reflections, or show some parallelism of perspectives of the real and reflected world. Another image that I would like to analyze here along with the selfie described above is Miguel Ángel Gaüeca's *Nobody Knows Vermeer Told Me This* (2004). The image depicts a person reading a handwritten letter, standing in front of a wall displaying four wall mounted mirrors, each of different sizes, in which the scene of reading is repeated. The scene in all mirrors side by side, as they hang, seems quite improbable as the scene that is depicted as reality is angled, while all the lines of the furniture appear straight.

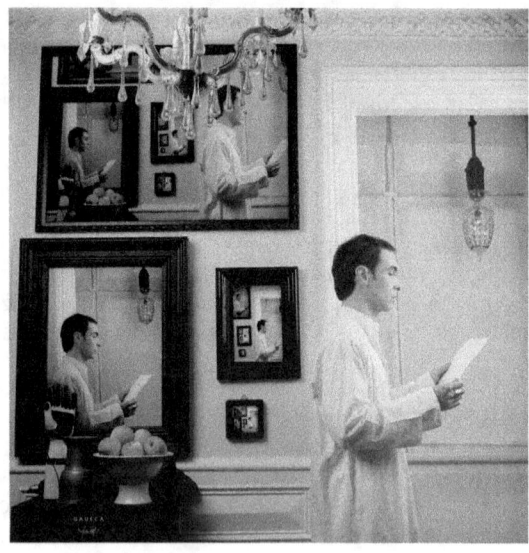

Image 19 – Miguel Ángel Gaüeca: *Nobody Knows Vermeer Told Me This* (2004, Collection of Coca Cola Foundation).

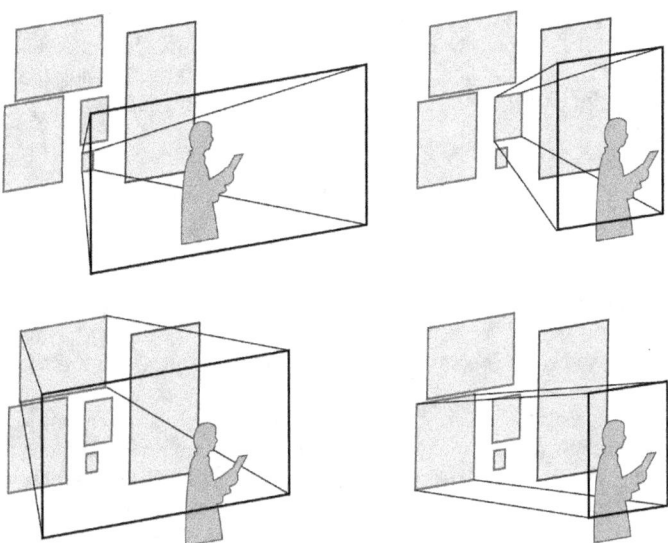

Graph 7 – Spacing in Gaüeca's *Nobody Knows Vermeer Told Me This*. The picture shows there are more mirrors present at the scene. These mirrors are not naturally set up but this is a photo-montage; the image is consisted of fully distorted depictions of the space.

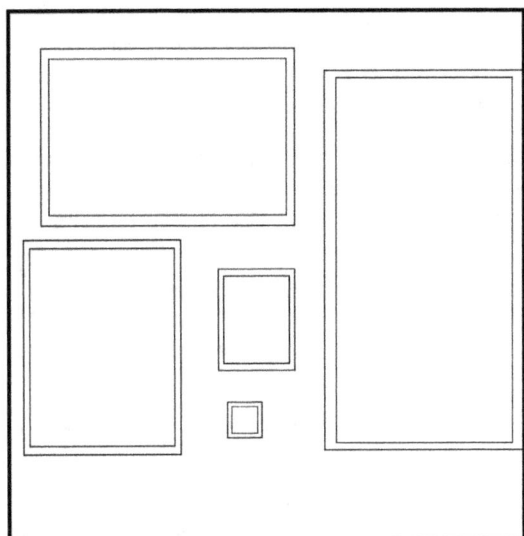

Graph 8 – Schema of representation of mirrors in Gaüeca's self-portrait.

Here, mirrored reality is inconsistent. Each of the frames on the wall shows a different reflection, first of all in framing a scene. The closest cut to the one that the viewer sees in the mirror is in the middle, to the right. Two mirrors show the most realist image; the largest mirror on the top and the smallest one that screens the widest view. While three mirrors catch a scene laid in front as straight, one of them produces the angled image. And it is precisely in this angled-view mirror that all horizontal lines of the image are straightened, while none of the vertical lines are. The vertical lines collapse in other mirrors too proving that the camera records from a point below the scene, a position that can be confirmed by shadows and angles of the portrait.

Only another mirror on the opposite side of the scene, our side, could have produced this total optical illusion of the multi-faceted reality, where mirrors are at the place where we, the viewers, as verifiers of the scene, stand. But, is that really what was happening in Vermeer's painting? Taking a look back at Vermeer's use of mirrors or, as some note, camera obscura, the device should appear behind the back of the viewer.[334] In that case, we should be visible too. Furthermore, the reality described would be much more consistent. The image is a set-up, not of reality but the media. The subtitle of the photograph also suggests a trick.

Contrary to Gaüeca's digital set-up, the image of the unknown selfie-maker from *The Selfie Olympics* is flat, brought up to the largest screen of the mirror in which everything sub-divides. While the selfie-maker is capable of controlling his mobile phone, he is hardly controlling the image on his notebook, depicting a less interesting angle than the one experimented in the artistic self-portrait.[335] Also, his depiction of virtual reality is not enigmatic the way Gaüeca's depiction is, as he simply stands confronting the mirror, while gazing into it.

'Portrait Anonyme'

The difference between the mirroring image and the mirrored reality is even more paradoxical in mirror-spectacles such as Magritte's *La reproduction Interdite* (1937). This 'painting is a painting' as the 'reflection is the reflection', is a circular visual definition, in a manner of *portrait anonym*, or the portrait of a person unwilling to reveal himself, such as in this portrait featuring the back of the commissioner, a certain Edward James.[336] James, shown from the back, is gazing into a mirror that paradoxically reflects his own back, instead of his face. As the angle of the mirror is not straight to the canvas, the frame presents the shelf of the fireplace in the lower-right position, on which significantly the book *The Narrative of Arthur Gordon Pym of Nantucket* by Edgar Allan Poe is placed, producing a perspective illusion.

---

334 Philip Steadman, *Vermeer's Camera: Uncovering the Truth Behind the Masterpieces*, Oxford: Oxford University Press, 2002.

335 One of the examples comes from the work by Lynda Benglis, *On Screen* (1972), showing the opposite of Magritte, namely herself enface, in front of the monitor that shows the very same image multiplied *ad infinitum*.

336 Enigmatic approach is, besides Gumpp's Self-Portrait Seen From the Back, present in Artemisia Gentileschi's Self-portrait as an Allegory of Painting (1630). Gentileschi portrays herself from the back, while painting. Still, in her left arm she holds the paint, while the right arm reaches in a space of the painting we do not see. Her personal space is dark, contrasted to her pale skin. Although it presumably looks like her, she performs the image described by Cesare Ripa: 'A beautiful woman, with full black hair, disheveled, and twisted in various ways, with arched eyebrows that show imaginative thought, the mouth covered with a cloth tied behind her ears, with a chain of gold at her throat from which hangs a mask, and has written in front "imitation". She holds in her hand a brush, and in the other the palette, with clothes of evanescently covered drapery.' Ripa via Christiansen. See: Keith Christiansen and Judith W. Mann, *Orazio and Artemisia Gentileschi*, New York and London: The Metropolitan Museum of Art and Yale University Press, 2001, p. 417.

While connotating Poe as the author of the symbolic and surreal atmosphere, the author of the painting, Magritte himself, is invisible. But, if James gazes at the mirror, should we not be able to see his face? As the painter sees him from the back, should he not be visible in the mirror too? And finally, if we are looking across the arm of James, should we be visible in the mirror too? This enigma occupied many art historians. Among others writing on the theme, Elkins noted:

> If a painting has a mirror, it may complicate matters by implying that the viewer does not exist as such – that the viewer is suddenly absent or transformed into someone else, as in self-portraits done in convex mirrors by Parmigianino, Andrea del Sarto, and others. And if such a painting also has "lookers" that return "our" gaze, the epistemology can become quite difficult to unravel.[337]

And in the case of *La Reproduction Interdite,* it is we, the viewers, who are segregated from Magritte, residing in different realities, it seems.[338] While James temporarily resides inside the painted scene, we are set outside of it, the very same place Magritte occupied while painting the scene; so, the position of the author, as the subject, and the position of the viewer collapse into each other. Yet one of these positions appears as timeless, while the other one temporary, in terms of values of time as length and duration. One, of the painter, belongs to the past, while the other of the audience belongs to the future. We see through the eyes of the painter, however, contrary to the selfie from The Selfie Olympics we do not see the author in the mirror.

While indeed anonymity existed in self-portraiture as well, in the manner of *Portrait Anonyme*, today's anonymity stands far from that classic genre. In Vermeer's *Allegory of Painting*, displaying the artist from the back, or Magritte's enigmatic portrait, as for example, some trace of the artist self-portraying remained, even when they turned their backs to their public.[339] But in contemporary anonymous self-portraits, we are forbidden to know what is hidden. While in Magritte's portrait the subject is shown, as well as the place of the missing artist and ourselves, in contemporary anonymous selfies, there is a substantial complementary and comparative part of information missing. While we can distinguish exclusion of the other from depicting self as the other, we cannot identify the person we do not know.

Photographic Miracle (of Subjects and Objects)

The medium plays a large role in the game of disappearance into the mirror. Magritte has set himself out of the painted picture, but he would not be able to set himself out of the photograph (and that is how we know Gaüeca's photograph is a photomontage). Maybe even the mirror Magritte faces across James' body, is not the mirror but the painting as well, for which reason, the author is invisible and irreproducible, as the title itself indicates.

Paintings are not obliged to reality. Yet, there are photographic portraits based on the same visual non-sense of the wrongly mirrored image. In a similar set-up of Joan Fontcuberta, the author takes the same place as Mr. James in Magritte's painting. During the time of his supposed stay at the fictional Valhamönde Monastery in Karelia, on the border of Finland

---

337 Elkins, *The Poetics of Perspective*, p. 118.
338 Similar constellation appears in Michelangelo Pistoletto's installations with mirrors.
339 Or even Danny Treacy's *Them* (2002), featuring a cross-dressing of the author's self-portrait, wearing different types of masks, forming genuine identities, such as clowns, Renaissance ladies etc.

and Russia, in which he claims to be given classes on magic, Fontcuberta often posed as an orthodox priest performing many 'miracles'.[340] In this particular wonder of the series, *Miracles&Co*, he stands in front of the mirror, dressed as a monk, holding a script on magic misattributed to King Solomon [lat. *clavicula Salomonis*] behind his back, once again underlining the mysticism of mirrors.[341] As in Magritte's portrait, instead of a face of a person in front of mirror being visible, his back is reflected into a large baroque mirror, under which there is a desk with a candle, imbuing mystical symbolism to the image. Being a photograph, this paradoxical self-portrait becomes even more confusing, as it is not possible to record oneself using photographic tools this way.

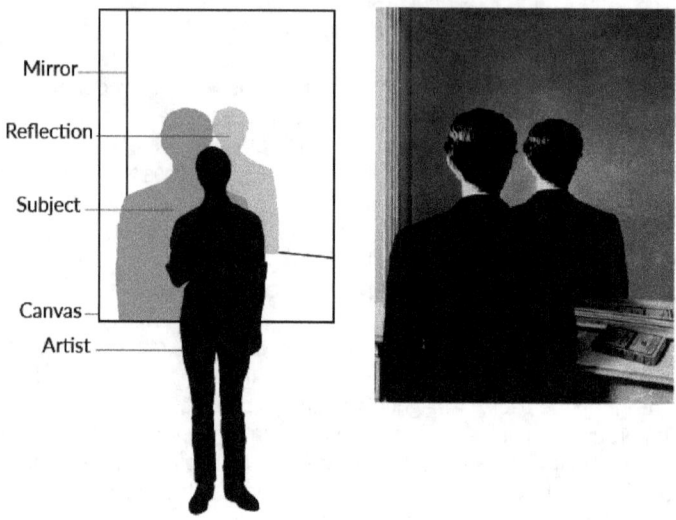

Graph 9 – Spacing in Magritte's *La Reproduction Interdite*, 1937.

This weird reality, however, is not the photographic one, as it is not technical, but rather a symbolic reality. The mirror takes the place of a mystical tool, producing an alternate mirrored reality. It is long believed to be the cursed space beyond-reality in which things, scarily enough, duplicate themselves. One reference to such reality goes directly from the title, referring to Carroll's *Behind the Looking Glass*, while the other more complex visual world of Magritte's *Reproduction*, or the one in Fontcuberta's painting where the viewer looks across the subject that throws the look back to the object's back.

---

340 In our e-mail conversation the author describes the space as 'isolated from the world by perpetual fog and by the labyrinth of the 13,710 islands of Lake Saimaa, the small monastic community of Valhamönde is inter-denominational and ecumenist, and monks from all the religions join that secret spiritual center to master the miracles techniques.'

341 The subtitle refers to Lewis Carroll, the author of *Through the Looking Glass and What Alice Found There* (1871), a fairytale based on the story of crossing to the inverted mirrored land Here.

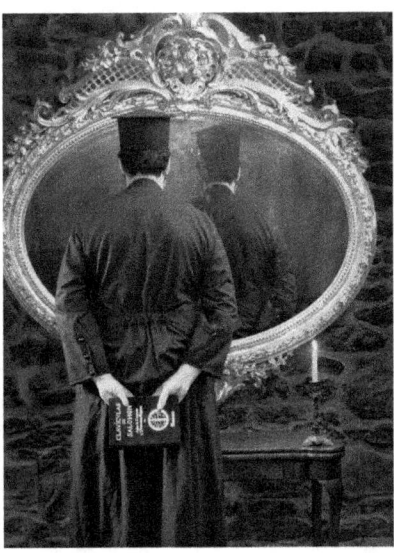

Image 20 – Joan Fontcuberta: The Miracle of the Mirror (Carroll Lewis, 2002).

Self-portrait and Portrait of the Self

Representative images, including photographs and realist paintings, define three spaces; the object's space, the author's space and the viewer's space, with a single reflection, each one looking across the back of the other. Still, these spaces are clashing in self-portraiture.[342] Self-portraits lay down a space seemingly objective in front of our subjective views, at the same time providing us someone's subjective attempt of objectification of self. It constructs an objective, outside view on one's own body, as in clinical death. Since the photographer becomes his own object, or turns objectified while giving his own, personal view as the subject, the subject-object loop thus constructed merges positions of the object and viewer. Holding a camera in hand, the objective space is projected onto the object, as the viewer simultaneously gazes into it. Viewers are set to view the scene from either the eyes of the author onto himself, or the eyes of someone else onto himself, in one case objectifying and on the other subjectifying oneself.

According to the distribution of the gaze, however, it is neither Magritte's painting nor Fontcuberta's photograph, nor is it Gaüeca's picture, being a self-portrait. Although using settlements of the mirror in the frontal manner, like the selfie from The Selfie Olympics does, Fontcuberta and Magritte offer a view through someone else's eyes that we cannot merely reconstruct from the image. We cannot reconstruct it from Gaüeca's picture either, as it shows the subject at the place of the object in a transparent way, depicting him while reading, not in the action of self-observing.

The self-portrait, contrary to portrait of the self, is a direct reflection that is made by a person situated in a continuous media loop with only himself. While the portrait of the self is a con-

---

342 Gardner, Annotated Alice.

clusive image, displaying what someone thinks and feels of himself, the self-portrait merely depicts a visual layout of the person. The portrait of the self is thus an internal reflection, while the self-portrait is the result of an external mirroring. Such difference of 'being made by' and 'representing' defines the beginning and the ending actions of the self in the representational order. One of these processes is irrational, subjective and compulsive, while the other rational, objective, and cognitive. One requires subjectivization, while the other requires objectification. Drawing a line of division of such mediations in media itself – it can be generalized – painting is the medium of the portrait of self, while photography of the self-portrait. Even photography may be used to make a portrait of the self in a painterly way, being mastered, as for example in the cases of Gaüeca's or Fontcuberta's pictures interpreting Magritte's visual paradox.

The second criterion for distinguishing the self-portrait from the portrait of the self, is in the immediacy of self-representation. While in self-depiction – because of a delay in classical photographic schema – it appears that even self-timed portraits are not the ideal self-portraits, as they produce a time-gap between recording and posing, as well as between shutting and developing the film, drawing a sharp line between two distinct ontological spaces; 'hereness' of perception and 'thereness' of the image. Sometimes distant gazing produces the great illusion of meeting someone, yet that person may never have been real, no matter how alive that view appears, as for example the Mona Lisa. Whereas, when the author depicts himself in a self-portrait, we are establishing a relationship to him. The author is not a neutral or subjective interpreter but he is – or he at least was – a living body that we are meeting with a time-delay. And, it was his intention that we meet in such a way.

Open and Closed Spaces

Changing positions from being in the centre of the space of the Renaissance, to being space itself in the period of modernism, in postmodern visual culture, the self seems to be caught in fatal collision between the inner and outer spaces.[343] The position of the object being painted or photographed necessarily is inside the frame of the picture, while the position of the subject interpreting, the author, exists only in the case of the self-portrait (and that is what makes the grammar of the image so interesting). Viewers, at the same time, can occupy both places; as a view on the outside space through the open window – defined by Alberti's open windows – and an inside space, which is continuous – defined by Andrea Pozzo – about a hundred years afterwards.[344] A perspective that builds the relationship of the subject's vision, framing his or her view onto the object, determines the position of the viewer, inside or outside of the image. To analyze such a position of the viewer, Brian Rotman has introduced the concept of *anteriority*, claiming the Renaissance has first found the viewer outside and then inside of the image, to finally deconstruct the whole concept of anteriority itself.[345]

Perspective in self-portraits, besides defining the place of the viewer, defines the place of the object and subject in the same person, allowing setting 'oneself in the distance,' taking

---

343 Regarding the Postmodern, Jay notes; 'If postmodernism teaches anything, however, it is to be suspicious of single perspective, which, like grand narratives, provide totalizing accounts of a world too complex to be reduced to a unified point of view.' Jay, *Downcast Eyes*, p. 545.

344 Andrea Pozzo, *Perspectiva pictorum et architectorum* (1642-1709) https://archive.org/details/gri_33125008639367.

345 Brian Rotman, *Signifying Nothing, The Semiotics of Zero*, New York: St. Martin's, Palgrave Macmillan, 1987.

space to see oneself, and paradoxically abandoning one's body. The moment we are facing someone, along with his subjective view on himself and usually inside his personal space, we are simultaneously being given a total illusion of the media cooling up the reality, in McLuhan's terms, presenting it as existing, thus, objective space in which this paradox occurs. While the author tries to objectify himself, by putting himself in perspective, he paradoxically subjectifies the space interpreted, making the self-portrait a unique genre of subject-object exchange and replacement.

This exchange becomes even more complex once the anticipated viewer comes into the image from the real into the virtual, photographic space of the image, tunnelling between the flat-world of two dimensions and the real world of four ones – it becomes 'plastic'. Crucial among processes, in the first dimension of the flat screen then becomes one of identification between self as subject and self as object, based on the recognition of self, as well as the identification between subject and object preceding their inter-subjective projection, or transfer, between the two in real space.

Space With no Gravity

A special place in perspective, here will be the one of 'vanishing point' taken as appearing around 1600 along with a mass of self-portraits and seen as metaphysical non-hereness (or; thereness) by many authors. Commonly this space was seen as death itself and, and it can be recognized, though not referred, in self-portraits with cadavers.

Bedtime selfies expose even larger flatness that resemble Medieval image. Their spaces are organized by symbolic order, rather than corresponding metrics, already a flat image. They are a corporeal, gestural, special, and, reusing perspective as an individualistic and accidental point of view.[346] For example, the image of the sleeper from The Selfie Olympics, exposing certain flatness, characteristic for the pre-perspective times. In the bedtime selfie, a half-naked man is acting as if he is asleep.[347] At the same time, while his bed is bare mattress without sheets, he is covered with a childish bed sheet featuring birds and butterflies. Funnily enough, he is holding a toy in one arm, and a mobile in the other. Further, he is attached to a doorframe with a sticker. As the door hanger is visible, besides the sticker, as well as the mirror's shelf with some other toy, it is clear that the guy is standing while self-recording. The flat perspective, mimicking a God's eye view is medieval, reminding one of the alternate origins of the image.[348]

---

346 Panofsky, *Perspective as Symbolic Form*.
347 A Bedtime selfie, http://knowyourmeme.com/photos/679129-selfie-olympics.
348 Besides visual flatness and the metaphysical 'bird view', accumulation of insignia in contemporary selfies also reminds us of Medieval iconographic building of images. In the selfie of a person with musical gadgets, for example, a guy poses with five different instruments, over-showing he is a musician, playing with accumulative symbolism as once employed in the presentations of Virgin Mary. A number of signs accumulating producing medieval *horror vacui*.

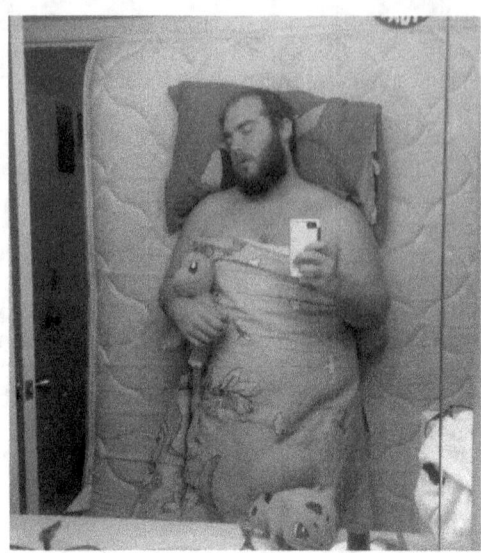

Image 21 – Image from Selfie-Olympics.

Amazingly enough, since the disappearance of the stable witness, these pictures remind us of medieval icons, with flat space, neutral faces and a number of objects flying around, formulating a rebus type of enigma that is supposed to speak for oneself. Reminding us of times when the self was not yet 'invented,' as neither their authors on the level of consciousness, these images draw back to the theme of *acheiropoieta*, self-generated images. Objects are hanging around similarly to attributes in medieval pictures, but now instead of pigeons of The Holy Spirit, roses of Virgin Mary, or slippers and the dog of the Arnolfini couple, there are toothbrushes, ring cookers and, guitars, serving as identifiers of the social position, age, race, and gender. These personal objects are symbolic insignia, similar to generic pillars, vases with flowers, and chairs from early portraiture.

Atelier, Studio, Photo-booth, Bathroom

What one can see in the presence of insignia is the advancement of capitalism from manufacturing to industrial type, from a space of 'living room capitalism', being neither private nor public, but showing-up, to a personal level of what can be named *toilet capitalism*, the intimacy of its frustrations. And this capitalism has no distinction whatsoever between private and public.

Visual media and technologies reorganize systems of power, primarily by reorganizing space descriptions, in terms of inner and outer space, viewer's space and body space, as well as their recourse. In reality, the first but surely most paradigmatic visualization of the system of control appeared in Plato's paradigm of cave from *Republica*.[349] Power in Plato's cave was organized inside-out. A controlled population is imprisoned inside a cave, while masters stay outside of the system. Bound with chains, slaves faced the walls of the cave, observing

---

349 Plato, *The Republic*, trans. Benjamin Jowett, retrieved from http://classics.mit.edu/Plato/republic.html.

shadows produced from a theatre behind their back, made in front of a fire as the light source. Agents of power imputed the ideology in playing with shadows.

With the rise of camera obscura, the inside-outside principle becomes more evident as the image from the outside of the camera came in, through a hole, and turned upside down.[350] Leonardo da Vinci described his vision of a new visual perfection in the representation of reality and in the not yet existing technology of image transfer.[351] According to Da Vinci's proposal, the viewer had to be positioned outside of the camera obscura system, consisting of a box with a tiny hole, through which a ray of light would be broken, transmitting the image on the surface of the opposite side.[352] The left-right orientation of the image was shown correctly; left side of the scene represented as the left side of the image, while the right one appeared at the right side of it. As the viewer stood outside of the system, he received a correct version of the object side-wise. The upside-down orientation however was twisted, producing a head downwards orientated image in regard to the scene viewed. Later, according to Athanasius Kircher in his work *Ars Magna Lucis et Umbrae* (1646), the painter's dream to develop a perfect tool, presented itself in the drawing of a gigantic tool for reproducing reality, in which a painter played a central part in the mechanism, becoming himself an inhabitant residing inside the optic system.[353] The image, as reflected in this model of the camera obscura, was flipped both left to right, as well as upside down.

Organization of power in a latter concept of control, the Panopticon, reflects the organizational plan of Plato's cave. The controlled population found themselves on the borders of the building, with a controlling agent in the middle.

In the 19th century, when the photographic camera was invented, portraits were taken inside the house and rarely outdoors. Cameras were huge and it was impracticable to carry them around along with tripods, at the beginning made of wood, but soon after becoming heavy metal pieces. To host the equipment, photo ateliers were spacey rooms, filled with different objects; chairs, armchairs, tables, pillars, vases with flowers, curtains and a lot of undistinguished draperies slipping from chairs, tables etc.

Some included costumes too. Victorian photographic studios were staged as living rooms in which deceased children were dressed up, selfies with cadavers are commonly shot at non-private and usually sterilized sites such as hospitals' autopsy departments, funeral sermons, and graveyards, on autopsies or at death ceremonies, making these portraits somehow impersonal. Such settlements served to simulate an upper-class society living room appearance for all customers, masking their real class and the use of their private space – although, photography was so expensive that it was hardly affordable to worker families.[354]

350 Sarah Kofman, *Camera Obscura of Ideology*, Ithaca and New York: Cornell University Press, 1999 (1973).
351 Broydrick E. Thro, 'Leonardo da Vinci's Solution to the Problem of the Pinhole Camera', *Archive for History of Exact Sciences* 48.3/4 (1994): 343-371.
352 Leonardo da Vinci, *The Codex Atlanticus*, 1478-1519.
353 Anamorphic magic lantern appeared in Athanasius Kirchner's *Mundus Subterraneus* (1664).
354 Pierre Bourdieu, Luc Boltanski, Robert Castel, Jean-Claude Chamboredon and Dominique Schnapper, *Photography: a Middle-Brow Art*, trans. Shaun Whiteside, Cambridge: Polity, 1998 (1965).

Gradually, as photography became more affordable and accessible to different social strata, 19th century visual narrative was abandoned. Places became smaller and functional studios replaced the classical ateliers.

What we name photographic portrait studio is a smaller place, having a certain industrial appearance rather than appearing like a cozy living room. Walls are commonly grey, sometimes even black, while instead of a number of smaller accessories, there were constructions for mounting different, usually printed, backdrops and backgrounds. Rudolf Arnheim described this setting of the portrait studio:

> A different social code protected both participants. The sitter, his spontaneity suspended and his best appearance displayed, has invited scrutiny. The amenities of intercourse are abrogated, there is no need for conversation, and the I is fully authorized to stare at the Thou as though it were an It. [...] The equipment was too bulky to catch anybody unawares, and the exposure time was long enough to wipe the accidents of the moment from face and gesture. Hence the enviable timelessness of the early photographs.[355]

The same century invented a peep show, originally being the generic name for any type of multi-participant observed through a hole.[356] Positioning the viewer outside the scene, rather than in the middle as in the Panopticon, peep shows gave physical freedom to observers.

Finally, the photo-booth is the paradigm of the closed space, invented at the beginning of the 20th century.[357] The photo-booth was a full self-service system, the same person was both photographer and object, filling up full run around the machine; starting it up at one place, posing at the other, and waiting for photographs at the outside. The most emancipated version of the visual prison was based on self-surveillance, a photo-booth, where the controlled one and the power instance, which controls are one and the same, as person moves from the inside towards the outside.[358]

The chain of production with a photo-booth becomes self-sufficient, and perfectly looped. Also, it was almost instant in recording and processing the image. This construct – not in fact knowing photography but doing it – has erased the presence of the photographer, merging personas of subject, object, commissioner, and the public.[359] The settlement has allowed much larger freedom of posing and playing.

The system was cheap, not including many elements of classical photography production, so photography became more available to masses. Finally, the world has faced new spurious

---

355 Rudolf Arnheim, 'On the Nature of Photography', *Critical Inquiry* 1.1 (1974): XX.

356 Crary, *Techniques of the Observer*.

357 It was precisely the time that can be marked with the invention of the first photo-booth, or *photomaton*, in 1924 or 1925. The photo-booth reminds us of the confessional booth. Aside the photo-booth, there were also other machines produced to make self-portraits, as for example *self* – a portrait machine that leads a person's head to draw his/her own portrait from the photograph measured by the machine, which is using facial recognition software.

358 The photo-booth was built around 1925 by Anatol M. Josepho. The device automated the processing of photography, constructing a closed system consisting of a light box, dark room, and delivery spot.

359 Reminding on well-known Searle's Chinese room argument. See: John R. Searle, 'Minds, Brains and Programs', *Behavioral and Brain Sciences* 3.3 (1980): 417-457.

images, as the technology was used in irrelevant occasions of passing nearby the box, not some grand events of life. The system produced a minimum of four shots in a row, which were sequenced. They had minor differences of grimaces, so photo-albums suddenly started to look like films, rather than a plausible narrative someone in the future can read.

New technologies of self-recording succeeding the photo-booth managed to displace, or even more radically, expel a subject from the box. Automatic and digital cameras are all excluding the photographer, but also the space from the production of the picture. Nevertheless, most selfies are recorded in small spaces, as in cars or other tiny places, any place with a mirror or reflective surface. Many of them are rather intimate locations, such as toilets and bathrooms, as if self-portraying is a perverse act *per se*. These places are all but neutral, and genuine as 19th century living rooms or gray boxes of photographic studios.

A deeper look can uncover many details of people's personal lives, first of which is a tiny bathroom, and the position of probably the only mirror in the apartment, that is used for self-portraying, as for example in the case of The Selfie Olympics in the beginning of this chapter.

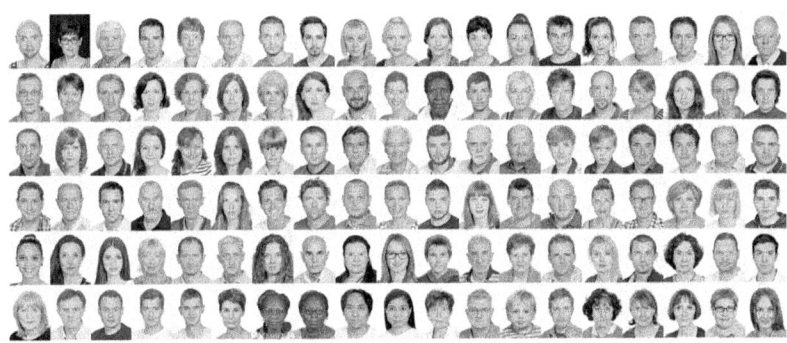

Image 22 – Passport photographs collage (2011/16, my photographs).

Privacy

Simultaneously, control in the online society is largely dependent on online presence and exhibitionism. 'Our society is not one of spectacle but of surveillance', Foucault once noted.[360] Self-portraits in general, selfies especially, can be approached from the perspective of privacy invasion, in regard to the objects' represented gaze, but also objects of a willing destruction of privacy. Henry A. Giroux writes, 'Privacy has become a curse, an impediment that subverts the endless public display of the self,' continuing with this quote by Bauman

> The area of privacy turns into a site of incarceration, the owner of private space being condemned and doomed to stew in his or her own juice; forced into a condition

---

360 Foucault, *Discipline and Punish*, p. 17.

marked by an absence of avid listeners eager to wring out and tear away the secrets from behind the ramparts of privacy.[361]

Still, the most problematic social element of the global obsessive self-reporting phenomena appears not regarding their picture's quality but rather their content – being over-exposure but also invasion of other people's privacy.[362] Subjects in the contemporary age lost their privacy.[363] Moreover, they are willing to self-expose it.[364] Susan Sontag noted many narcissists use self-surveillance as a method.[365]

There are plenty of examples of artists stripping in front of the surveillance eye, as for example in performances of artists Tomislav Gotovac or Vlasta Delimar, giving up their privacy in the form of their naked performances, or Polish artist Július Koller, who is maybe the most systematic in his self-display against control.[366] Koller's work speaks of the claustrophobia of silence, of a mad asylum produced by the events around the 1968 mass student demonstrations in Poland. Since that particular political moment, the author literally escapes into the self-sufficient universe, containing elements of fiction, often referring to *Cosmohumanist Culture*, two years later introducing the UFO (Universal-Cultural Futurological Operations), since when his self-portraits are called *U.F.O.-naut J.K.*[367]

---

361 Henry A. Giroux, 'America's Addiction to Terrorism', *Monthly Review Press*, 2015, p. 157.
362 Many embarrassing selfies show other people in the second plan, as for example a grandmother asleep, people in the hospital, worried parents, abandoned and bored children, dead bodies at funerals, cops stopping cars and people on the toilet, see '34 Embarrassing Selfie Fails, #18 is the Most Awkward Thing I've Ever Seen', http://www.lifebuzz.com/selfie-fail/.
363 The loss of privacy of the object recorded, as well as a distribution of private photographs – both breaking traditional photography ethics – hit the climax in criminal practices of privacy invasion, by photo and video stalking of paparazzi, but also in illegal recording and distributing images of children photographs. The loss of sanctity of the private space permitted recording people while eating or sitting on toilet, followed by a rise of sadistic mass culture, transgressing the old professional confidentiality norms of photographic ateliers. Accompanied with the massive distribution and a loss of bound of confidentiality and protection of privacy, photography is slowly invading the boundaries and limits of the others. For the legality of photographs see early discussions; 'Privacy, Photography, and the Press', *Harvard Law Review* 111 (1998); and Mensel RE 'Kodakers Lying in Wait: Amateur Photography and the Right of Privacy in New York', *American Quarterly* 43 (1991).
364 Some images also push the personal into the public space, as a guy sitting on a construction of glasses, stacked directly into his anus, or one shooting with a mobile phone with his anal muscles, provoking even more than once scandalous naked Robert Mapplethorpe ever did.
365 Funnily enough, Jeremy Bentham, inventor of the Panopticon, has been among the ones delivering their corpse to anatomic dissection to public schools, in order to pass England's Anatomy Act in 1832. His body is still displayed at the University College, made out of wax, cast upon his own instruction. This 'auto-icon' as Klaver names it, 'is an attempt on Bentham's part to eradicate the space between oneself and the image of oneself by making the subject, or at least the subject's remains, an essential ingredient in the representation of the subject.' Klaver, *Sites of Autopsy in Contemporary Culture*, p. 20.
366 Exhibition Július Koller, '?' Museum of Contemporary Art, Warsaw, 25 September 2015 – 10 January 2016 Complete oeuvre of Koller's work is literary self-preoccupied, but not self-obsessed. There is a visible lack of narcissist posture, in terms of performativity towards oneself, contrary to feminist artist on the west, from the very same time. Koller even looks very shy.
367 Many of the pictures of the self are marked with a question mark, appearing as a sign of the unknown, as a UFO is. The UFO sign speaks both on the political instability of 1968 in Poland, as well as personal identity.

Still, it is a dilemma of the contemporary age that the paranoid has illusions of self-importance; exhibitionism and paranoia are just two sides of the same coin. Easily distributed digital photographs are crossing barriers of privacy, as leaked scandals.[368] While on the one hand there is a whole movement of the Anonymous, inventing masks to cover up their own identity in public spaces or events, on the other there is an urge to uncover specificities to the same society, to unveil and strip.[369] This exposure of personal space or invading someone else's territory, used to be monitored by professional photographers working as laboratory workers, or in the myth by stalking Echo. They used to be inter-mediators as well as censors of reality, as customers were self-censoring.

Without inter-mediators and witnesses, it is the reality transmitted without experience, as being behind one's back, strangely enough, while looking at one's own self. This mediated reality like tourist selfies showing monuments in the second plane, dead bodies featured on cadaver selfies, the scary abyss seen behind the heads of roof selfie makers, is not an experience captured, as creating a real object's space, does not exist as such. It has become merely a world constructed and represented; the world subjected without ever being lived. It could have been wallpapers behind their back too. How would they know the difference?

---

368 Bernhard Porksen and Hanne Detel, *The Unleashed Scandal: The End of Control in the Digital Age*, Imprint Academic, 2014.
369 Aside Guy Fawkes there is yet another mask used for disinfection of identity. See: Leslie Katz, 'Anti-surveillance mask lets you pass as someone else', *CNet*, 8 May 2014, http://www.cnet.com/news/urme-anti-surveillance-mask-lets-you-pass-as-someone-else/.

BIBLIOGRAPHY

'34 Embarrassing Selfie Fails, #18 Is The Most Awkward Thing I've Ever Seen', *LifeBuzz*, http://www.lifebuzz.com/selfie-fail/.

'A Bedtime selfie', *Know Your Meme*, 2014, http://knowyourmeme.com/photos/679129-selfie-olympics.

Alpers, Svetlana. 'Interpretation Without Representation, or, the Viewing of Las Meninas', *Representations* 1 (February, 1983): 30-42.

Aristotle, 'De Insomniis', in Jonathan Barnes (ed), *The Complete Works of Aristotle*, Princeton: Princeton University Press, 1984, at 459b24-460a32 (459b28-460a18).

Alberti, *De Pictura* (1435), http://www.noteaccess.com/Texts/Alberti/.

Arnheim, Rudolf. 'On the Nature of Photography', *Critical Inquiry* 1.1 (1974): 149-161, Princeton: Princeton University Press, 1984, 459b24-460a32 (459b28-460a18).

Bal, Mieke. *Looking in: The Art of Viewing*, Critical Voices in Art, Theory and Culture, London: Routledge, Taylor and Francis, 2004.

Barthes, Roland. *The Pleasure of the Text*, trans. Richard Miller, New York: Hill and Wang, Farrar, Strauss and Giroux, 1975.

_____. *Camera Lucida: Reflections on Photography,* trans. Richard Howard, New York: Hill and Wang, 2000 (1980).

_____. Roland Barthes, trans. Richard Howard, London and Basingstoke: Macmillan Press, 1977.

Bataille, Georges. *Story of the Eye*, London: Penguin Classics, 2001 (1928).

Baudrillard, Jean. *Selected writings*, Redwood City: Stanford University Press, 2002.

Bazin, André. 'The Ontology of Photographic Image', *Film Quarterly* 13.4 (1960): 4-9.

Belting, Hans. *An Anthropology of Images. Picture, Medium, Body,* Princeton and Oxford: Princeton University Press, 2011.

Benjamin, Walter. 'A Short History of Photography', in Allan Trachtenberg (ed.) *Classic essays on photography,* New Haven, Conn.: Leete's Island Books, 1980 (1931): 199-216.

_____. 'The Work of Art in the Age of Mechanical Reproduction', in Francis Frascina, Charles Harrison et. al (eds) *Modern Art and Modernism: A Critical Anthology*, London: Paul Chapman & Open University, 1982 (1936): 217-221.

Berger, John. *Ways of Seeing*, London: Penguin books, 1972.

_____. 'Embrace', https://www.youtube.com/watch?v=Obt2nSQ2Ud0.

Bergstein, Mary. *Mirrors of Memory: Freud, Photography and the History of Art*, Ithaca and London: Cornell University Press, 2010.

Blackburn, Simon. *Mirror, Mirror: The Uses and Abuses of Self Love*, Princeton and Oxford: Princeton University Press, 2014.

Blanchot, Maurice and Derrida, Jacques. *The Instant of my Death: Demeure (Fiction and Tesimony)*, trans. Elizabeth Rottenberg, Meridian Crossing Aesthetics Series, Stanford: Stanford University Press, 2000.

Boccaccio, Giovanni. *Des claires et nobles femmes*, trans. by Laurent de Premierfait, Paris: Bibliothèque Nationale de France, 1402.

Bourdieu, Pierre, Luc Boltanski, Robert Castel, Jean-Claude Chamboredon and Dominique Schnapper, *Photography: A Middle-Brow Art,* trans. Shaun Whiteside, Cambridge: Polity, 1998 (1965).

Brant, Sebastian S. *Ship of Fools*, New York: Dover Publications, 2011 (1494).

Buffardi, Laura L. and Campbell, Keith W. 'Narcissism and Social Networking Web Sites', *Personality and Social Psychology Bulletin* 34.10 (2008): 1303-1314, DOI: 10.1177/0146167208320061.

Buse, Peter. *The Camera does the rest*, Chicago: University of Chicago Press, 2016.

Cadava, Eduardo. 'Words of light: Theses on the Photography as History', *Diacritics* 22.3/4 (1992): 85-114.

Campany, David. *Art and Photography, Times and Movements*, London: Phaidon, 2007.

Carlton Natalie R. 'Digital culture and art therapy', *The Arts in Psychotherapy* 41 (2014): 41-45.

Carpenter, Christopher. 'Narcissism on Facebook, Self-promotional and Anti-Social Behavior', *Personality and Individual Differences*, 52.4 (2012): 482-486.

Chesne, Joseph du. *Le Grand Miroir du Monde*, 1587, http://gallica.bnf.fr/ark:/12148/bpt6k5860952d.r=Le+grand+miroir+du+monde.langFR.

Christiansen, Keith and Mann, Judith W. *Orazio and Artemisia Gentileschi*, New York, New Heaven, and London: The Metropolitan Museum of Art and Yale University Press, 2001.

Chumley, Cheryl K. and Boyer, Dave. 'Obama Takes Selfie at Mandela's Funeral Service', *The Washington Times*, 10 December 2013, http://www.washingtontimes.com/news/2013/dec/10/obama-takes-selfie-mandelas-funeral-service/.

Crary, Jonathan. *Techniques of the Observer. On Vision and Modernity in the Nineteenth Century*, Cambridge and London: MIT Press, 1992.

_____. 'Spectacle, Attention, Counter-Memory', *October* 50 (1989): 96-107, http://my.ilstu.edu/\~jk-shapi/Crary%20Spectacle.pdf.

Criminisi, Antonio, Martin Kemp and Sing B. Kang. 'Reflections of Reality in Jan van Eyck and Robert Campin', *Historical Methods: A Journal of Quantitative and Interdisciplinary History* 27.3 (2004): 99-122, DOI: 10.3200/HMTS.37.3.

Crozier, W. Ray and Greenhalgh, Paul. 'Self-Portraits as Presentations of Self', *Leonardo* 21.1 (1988): 29-33.

Damisch, Hubert. *The Origin of Perspective*, trans. John Goodman, Cambridge and London: MIT Press, 1995 (1987).

Danto, Arthur. 'The Naked Truth', in Scott Walden (ed), *Photography and Philosophy: Essays on the Pencil of Nature*, New Jersey: Blackwell Publishing, 2008, 284-309.

'Death in Harlem', *CNN*, 24 April 2014, http://edition.cnn.com/2014/04/24/living/gallery/vander-zee-death/index.html.

Dennett, Daniel. *Consciousness Explained,* New York: Back Bay Books, 1992.

Derrida, Jacques. *Copy, Archive, Signature: A Conversation on Photography,* trans. Jeff Fort, Stanford: Stanford University Press, 2010.

_____. *Memoirs of the Blind: The Self-Portrait and Other Ruins*, trans. Pascale-Anne Brault and Michael Naas, Chicago and London: University of Chicago Press, 1993.

_____. *The Gift of Death*, trans. David Wills, 2nd Edition & Literature in Secret (Religion and Postmodernism), Chicago and London: University of Chicago Press, 1996 (1992).

Descartes, René. *Meditations on First Philosophy*. trans. Elizabeth S. Haldane, Cambridge: Cambridge University Press, 1911, http://selfpace.uconn.edu/class/percep/DescartesMeditations.pdf.

Dewey, Caitlin. 'The Other Side of Infamous Aushwitz Selfie', *Washington Post*, 22 July 2014, https://www.washingtonpost.com/news/the-intersect/wp/2014/07/22/the-other-side-of-the-infamous-aus-chwitz-selfie/.

Dewey, John. *Experience and Nature*, Carbondale: Southern Illinois University Press, 1988.

Didi-Huberman, Georges. *Invention of Hysteria: Charcot and the Photographic Iconography of the Salpêtrière*, trans. Alisa Hartz, Cambridge/London: MIT Press, 2003.

Doy, Gen. *Picturing the Self: Changing View on the Subject in Visual Culture*, London: I. B. Tauris, 2005.

Durando, Jessica. 'Auschwitz Selfie Girl Defends her Action', *USA today*, 23 July 2014, https://www.usatoday.com/story/news/nation-now/2014/07/23/selfie-auschwitz-concentration-camp-germa-ny/13038281/.

_____. 'Auschwitz Selfie Girl Breanna Mitchell Defends her Controversial Picture", *The Huffington Post*, 24 July 2014, http://www.huffingtonpost.com/2014/07/24/auschwitz-selfie-girl-breanna-mitch-ell_n_5618225.html.

Duve, Thierry de. 'Time Exposure and Snapshot: The Photograph as Paradox', *October* 5 (Summer, 1978): 113-125.

Eco, Umberto. *Limits of Interpretation (Advances in Semiotics Series)*, Bloomington and Indianapolis: Indiana University Press, 1991.

Elkins, James. *The Poetics of Perspective*, Ithaca and London: Cornell University Press, 1996.

Flusser, Vilém. *Towards a Philosophy of Photography,* London: Reaktion, 2000.

_____. *Into the Universe of Technical Images*, Minneapolis and London: University of Minnesota Press, 2011.

Foucault, Michel. *Culture of the Self*, Lectures at UC Berkeley, http://www.openculture.com/2014/08/michel-foucaults-lecture-the-culture-of-the-self.html.

_____. *Discipline and Punish*, New York: Vintage Books, 1995 (1975).

_____. 'Technologies of the Self', in Martin Luther H., Huck Gutman, and Patrick H. Hutton (eds.), *Technologies of the Self: A Seminar with Michel Foucault,* London: Tavistock Publications and The University of Massachusetts Press, 1988.

_____. *The Order of Things*, New York: Pantheon Books, 1970 (1966).

Freud, Sigmund. *Introductory lectures on psycho-analysis*, pt. III, Hogarth Press and the Institute of Psycho-Analysis, 1963.

Fromm, Erich. *The Heart of Man*, New York: Lantern Books, 2010 (1964).

Frosh, Paul. 'The Gestural Image. The Selfie, Photography Theory and Kinesthetic Sociability', *International Journal of Communication* 9 (2015): 1607-1628, DOI: 1932–8036/2015FEA0002.

Gallese, Vittorio and Goldman, Al. 'Mirror Neurons and the Simulation Theory of Mind-Reading', *Trends in Cognitive Sciences* 12.2 (1998): 493-501, DOI: 10.1016/s1364-6613(98)01262-5.

Gardner, Martin and Carroll, Lewis. *The Annotated Alice. Alice's Adventures in Wonderland and Through the Looking Glass by Lewis Carroll*, illustr. John Tenniel, New York: Wings Books, 1993 (1960).

Getty Museum. 'Hyppolite Bayard', http://www.getty.edu/art/collection/artists/1840/hippolyte-ba-yard-french-1801-1887/.

Gide, Andre. *Traktat o Narcisu. Teorija simbola.* Zagreb: AGM, 2003 (1891).

Giroux, Henry A. *America's Addiction to Terrorism.* Monthly Review Press, 2016.

_____. 'Selfie Culture in the Age of Corporate and State Surveillance', *Third Text* 29.3 (2015): 155-164, DOI: 10.1080/09528822.2015.1082339.

Gleig, Ann. 'The Culture of Narcissism Revised, Transformations of Narcissism in Contemporary Psychospirituality', *Pastoral Psychology* 59 (2010), DOI: 10.1007/s11089-009-027-9.

Goodwin, Sarah Webster and Bronfen, Elizabeth (eds) *Death and Representation, (Parallax: Re-visions of Culture and Society Series),* Baltimore: Johns Hopkins University Press, 1993.

Greenblatt, Stephen. *Renaissance Self-Fashioning,* Chicago: University of Chicago Press, 1980.

Groys, Boris. *Dream Factory Communism,* Berlin: Hatje Cantz Publishers, 2003.

Hall, James. *The Self-Portrait: A Cultural History,* London: Thames and Hudson, 2014.

Hannavy, John. *Encyclopedia of Nineteenth-Century Photography,* New York and London: Routledge, 2008.

Harvey, John. *Photography and Spirit,* London: Reaktion Books, 2007.

Hayles, Katherine. *How we Became Posthuman: Virtual Bodies in Cybernetics, Literature, and Informatics,* Chicago and London: University of Chicago Press, 1999.

Rimke, Heidi. 'The Culture of Therapy: Psychocentrism in Everyday Life', in M. Thomas (ed.) *Power and Everyday Practices,* Toronto: Nelson, 2012, pp. 182-202.

Hershenson, Maurice. *Visual Space Perception: A Primer,* Cambridge and London: Bradford Book and MIT Press, 1999.

Hockney, David and Falco, Charles M. 'Optical insight into Renaissance', *Art, Optics & Photonics News* 11.7 (2000): 52-59, DOI: 10.1364/OPN.11.7.000052.

International Journal of Communication, http://ijoc.org/.

'"I wouldn't do anything differently": Teen who took selfie at Auschwitz is unrepentant as trend for grinning and pouting poses at memorials including Ground Zero grows', *Daily Mail Online,* 23 July 2014, http://www.dailymail.co.uk/news/article-2702161/I-wouldnt-differently-Teenager-took-selfie-Auschwitz-unrepentant-trend-posing-memorials-including-Ground-Zero-grows.html.

Jay, Martin. *Downcast Eyes: The Denigration of Vision in Twentieth-Century French Thought,* Berkeley and Los Angeles: California University Press, 1994.

Jauregui, Andres. 'Gravedigger Suspended After Taking Photo With Exhumed Body', *The Huffington Post,* 13 September 2014, http://www.huffingtonpost.com/2014/09/13/gravedigger-photo-dead-body_n_5810300.html.

Jerman, Željko. *Moja godina 1977,* Zagreb: SCCA, 1997.

Jones, Amelia. *Self-Image, Technology, Representation and the Contemporary Subject,* London: Routledge Taylor and Francis, 2006.

_____.'The "Eternal Return": Self-Portrait Photography as a Technology of Embodiment', *Signs* 27.4 (2002): 947-978.

Jo Spence, http://www.jospence.org/.

Kalmanowitz, Debra and Potash, Jordan S. 'Ethical Considerations in the Global Teaching and Promotion of art Therapy to Non-Art Therapists', *The Arts in Psychotherapy* 37 (2010): 20-26.

Katz, Leslie. 'Anti-surveillance Mask Lets you Pass as Someone Else', *CNet,* 8 May 2014, http://www.cnet.com/news/urme-anti-surveillance-mask-lets-you-pass-as-someone-else/.

Kismaric, Susan. '*Self-Portrait: The Photographer's Persona*, 1840-1985, *MoMA* 37 (Autumn, 1985): 5.

Khayyam, Omar. *The Rubaiyat*, 1120 A.C.E, http://classics.mit.edu/Khayyam/rubaiyat.html.

Klaver, Elisabeth. *Sites of Autopsy in Contemporary Culture*, New York: SUNY Series in Postmodern Culture, 2005.

Kofman, Sarah. *Camera Obscura of Ideology*, Ithaca and New York: Cornell University Press, 1999 (1973).

Kozloff, Max. *The Theatre of the Face: Portrait Photography Since 1900,* London and NewYork: Phaidon, 2007.

Kracauer, Siegfried. *Theory of Film: The Redemption of Physical Reality*, New Jersey: Princeton University Press, 1997 (1969).

Krauss, Rosalind. 'Video: The Aesthetics of Narcissism', *October* 1 (Spring, 1976): 50-64.

_____. *Optical Unconsciousness*, Cambridge: MIT Press, 1993.

_____. 'The Photographic Conditions of Surrealism', *October 19* (1981): 3-34.

Kristeva, Julia. *Powers of Horror: An Essay on Abjection,* trans. Celine Louis Ferdinand, New York: University of Columbia Press, 1982.

Lacan, Jacques. *Mirror Stage*, Lecture at Fourteenth International Psychoanalytical Congress at Marienbad, 1936.

Lasch, Christopher. *The Culture of Narcissism: American Life in an Age of Diminishing Expectations*, New York and London: W. W. Norton & Company, 1991 (1979).

Lefebvre, Henri. *Production of the Space,* trans. Donald Nicholson-Smith, New Jersey and Oxford, Wiley-Blackwell, 1992.

Leibniz, Gottfried Wilhelm. *The Principles of Philosophy Known as Monadology*, 1714, http://www.earlymoderntexts.com/assets/pdfs/leibniz1714b.pdf.

Loewenberg, Ina. 'Reflections on Self-Portraiture in Photography', *Feminist Studies* 25 (1999): 398-408.

Loewenthal, Del. *Phototherapy and Therapeutic Photography in a Digital Age*, London and New York: Routledge, 2013.

Lovink, Geert. *Zero Comments: Blogging and Critical Internet Culture*, New York and London: Routledge, 2008.

Manovich, Lev. 'Subjects and Styles in Instagram Photography', *Manovich*, http://manovich.net/index.php/projects/subjects-and-styles-in-instagram-photography-part-1.

Martin, Raymond and Barresi, John. 'Inhabiting the Image: Photography, Therapy and Re-enactment', *European Journal of Psychotherapy and Counseling* 11.1 (2009): 35-49.

_____. *The Rise and Fall of Soul and Self: An Intellectual History of Personal Identity,* Ithaca and London: Columbia University Press, 2010.

Maurice Merleau-Ponty. *The Visible and the Invisible*. trans. Alphonso Lingis. Evanston: Northwestern University Press, 1968.

McLuhan, Marshall. *Understanding Media. The Extensions of Man*, intro. Lewis H. Lapham, Cambridge: MIT Press, 1994.

Mehdizadeh, Soraya. 'Self-Presentation 2.0: Narcissism and Self-Esteem on Facebook', (2010). *Cyberpsychology, Behavior, and Social Networking* 13.4 (2010): 357-364. DOI:10.1089/cyber.2009.0257.

Mensel, Robert E. 'Kodakers Lying in Wait: Amateur Photography and the Right of Privacy in New York, 1885-1915', *American Quarterly* 43 (1991).

Melchior-Bonnet, Sabine. *The Mirror: A History,* trans. Katherine H. Jewett, pref. Jean Delumeau London and New York: Routledge, Taylor and Francis, 2006.

Merleau-Ponty, Maurice. *The Visible and the Invisible*, trans. Alphonso Lingis, Evanston: Northwestern University Press, 1968.

Mirzoeff, Nicolas. *How to see the World*, London: Penguin Books, 2015.

Molloy, Antonia. 'Danny Bowman Taking Approximately 200 Photos a day, and Finally Becoming Suicidal After not Managing to Make "The Perfect one"', *The Independent*, 24 March 2014, http://www.independent.co.uk/news/uk/home-news/selfie-obsession-made-teenager-danny-bowman-suicid-al-9212421.html.

Moran, Lee. 'Alabama Girl Gets Death Threads After Taking Selfie at Auscwhitz', *NY Daily News*, 25 July 2014, http://www.nydailynews.com/news/national/alabama-girl-death-threats-selfie-auschwitz-ar-ticle-1.1879908.

Mosher, Michael A. 'The Judgmental Gaze of European Women: Gender, Sexuality, and the Critique of Republican Rule', *Political Theory* 22 (1994): 25-44, DOI:10.1177/0090591794022001003.

Muri, Simone Alter. 'Beyond the Face: Art Therapy and Portraiture', *The Arts in Psychotherapy* 34 (2007): 331-339.

Nair, Meghna. 'Selfitis: An Obsessive Compulsive Disorder of Taking too Many Selfies', *Newsgram*, 29 June 2015, http://www.newsgram.com/selfitis-an-obsessive-compulsive-disorder-of-taking-too-ma-ny-selfies/.

Nancy, Jean Luc. *Being Singular Plural,* Broadway: Stanford University Press, 2000.

Nedelcu, Elena and Nedelcu, Andra. 'The Exploration of the Self in Pictures: Photo-Therapy', *Challenges of the Knowledge Society* 25 (2012): 1842-1947.

Noland, Carrey M. 'Auto-Photography as Research Practice: Identity and Self-Esteem Research', *Journal of Research Practice* 2.1 (2006): 1-19, http://files.eric.ed.gov/fulltext/EJ805685.pdf.

Nuñez, Cristina. 'The Self Portrait, a Powerful Tool for Self-Therapy', *European Journal of Psychotherapy & Counselling* 11 (2009): 51-61, DOI: 13642530902723157.

Panofsky, Erwin. P*erspective as Symbolic Form*, trans. Christopher S. Wood, New York: Zone Books, 1991 (1927).

_____. 'Jan van Eyck's Arnolfini Portrait', *The Burlington Magazine for Conoisseurs* 64.372 (1934): 117-119; 122-127.

Peraica, Ana. *Fotografija kao Dokaz*, PhD diss., Faculty of Humanist and Social Sciences, University of Rijeka, Rijeka/Croatia, 2010.

_____. *Victims Symptom: PTSD and Culture*, Amsterdam: Institute of Network Cultures, 2009.

Peters, John Durham, *Speaking Into the Air: A History of the Idea of Communication*, Chicago: University of Chicago Press, 1999.

Phillips, Sandra S. and Baker, Simon. *Exposed: Voyeurism, Surveillance, and the Camera Since 1870*, London: Yale University Press, 2010.

Porksen, Bernhard and Detel, Hanne. *The Unleashed Scandal: The End of Control in the*

Digital Age, Imprint Academic, 2014.

Pozzo, Andrea, *Perspectiva pictorum et architectorum* (1642-1709). https://archive.org/details/gri_33125008639367.

'Privacy, Photography, and the Press', *Harvard Law Review* 111 (Feb, 1998).

Rimke, Heidi. 'The Culture of Therapy: Psychocentrism in Everyday Life', in M. Thomas (ed.) *Power and Everyday Practices*, Toronto: Nelson, 2012, 182-202.

Ripa, Cesare. *Iconologia, or, Moral Emblems* 1709, https://archive.org/details/iconologiaormora00ripa.

Rotman, Brian. *Signifying Nothing: The Semiotics of Zero*, New York: Palgrave Macmillan, 1987.

Rush, Michael. *Video Art*, London: Thames and Hudson, 2007.

Sánchez Cantón, Francisco Javier. *Las Meninas Y Sus Personajes,* Barcelona: Editorial Juventud, 1943.

Sass, Louis A. 'Introspection, Schizophrenia, and the Fragmentation of Self Representations', *Representations* 19 (1987): 1-34.

Sawday, Jonathan. *The Body Emblazoned: Dissection and the Human Body in Renaissance*, Florence: Taylor and Francis, 2013.

Schechner, Sara J. 'Between Knowing and Doing: Mirrors and Their Imperfections in the Renaissance', *Early Science and Medicine* 10.2, (2005): 137-162.

Schiller, Jakob. 'Wired: 10 Best Selfies from Selfie Olympics', *Wired*, 1 October 2014, http://www.wired.com/2014/01/the-10-best-photos-from-the-selfie-olympics/.

Schwartz, Hillel. *Culture of the Copy: Striking Likenesses, Unreasonable Facsimiles*, New York: Zone Books, 1996.

Searle, John R. "Las Meninas' and the Paradoxes of Pictorial Representation', *Critical Inquiry* 6.3 (1980): 477-488.

_____. 'Minds, Brains and Programs', *Behavioral and Brain Sciences* 3.3 (1980): 417–57.

Brant, Sebastian. *Ship of Fools*, Dover Publications, 2011 (1494).

Saint-Gobain, https://www.saint-gobain.com/en/group/our-history.

Sekula, Allan. 'The Body and the Archive', *October* 39 (Winter, 1986): 3-64.

Selfeey, http://selfeey.com/selfie-olympics.

Selfiecity, http://selfiecity.net/.

Selfie Research Network, http://www.selfieresearchers.com/.

Shanken, Edward. 'Virtual Perspective and the Artistic Vision: A Genealogy of Technology, Perception and Power', Rotterdam: ISEA, 1996.

Silverman, Hugh J. 'Cezanne's Mirror Phase', in Johnson Galen A. (ed) *The Merleau-Ponty Aesthetics Reader: Philosophy and Painting,* Evanston: Northwestern University Press, 1993.

Sontag, Susan. *On Photography,* New York: Farrar, Straus and Giroux, 1977.

_____. *Regarding the Pain of Others*, New York: Picador, Farrar Strauss and Giroux, 2003.

Steadman, Philip. *Vermeer's Camera: Uncovering the Truth Behind the Masterpieces*, Oxford: Oxford University Press, 2002.

Steinberg, Leo. 'Velázquez' "Las Meninas"', *October* 19 (1981): 45-54.

Styles, Ruth. 'Is This the World's First Amateur Selfie? Woman Captured her own Image in 1900 with Kodak Box Brownie Camera', *Daily Mail*, 19 November 2013, http://www.dailymail.co.uk/femail/article-2509952/Black-white-selfies-dating-1800s-shed-light-history-self-portrait.html.

Talbot, William H.F., *The Pencil of Nature*, Project Gutenberg, 2010 (1845).

Tembeck, Tamar. 'Exposed Wounds: The Photographic Autopathographies of Hannah Wilke and Jo Spence' *RACAR* XXXIII (2008): 87-101.

'The Oxford Dictionaries Word of the Year 2013', *Oxford Dictionaries*, 19 November 2013, http://blog.oxforddictionaries.com/press-releases/oxford-dictionaries-word-of-the-year-2013/.

'Therapeutic Photography' https://phototherapy-centre.com/therapeutic-photography/.

Thro, E. Broydrick. 'Leonardo da Vinci's Solution to the Problem of the Pinhole Camera', *Archive for History of Exact Sciences* 3/4 (1994): 343-371.

Vasari, Giorgio. *The Lives of the Artist*, Oxford: Oxford University Press, 1991 (c1550).

Vinci, Leonardo da. *The Codex Atlanticus,* 1478-1519, http://www.leonardodigitale.com/index.php?lang=ENG.

_____. *Notebooks*, Oxford: Oxford University Press, 2008: 212.

Wade, Kimberley A., Garry Maryanne, Don Read and Stephen Lindsay. 'A Picture is Worth a Thousand Lies: Using False Photographs to Create False Childhood Memories', *Psychonomic Bulletin & Review* 9 (2002): 597-603.

Walker-Rettberg, Jill. *Seeing Ourselves through Technology, London*: Palgrave Macmillan, 2014.

Walton, Kendall. 'Transparent Pictures: On the Nature of Photographic Realism', *Critical Inquiry* 11 (1984): 246-277.

Warburton. Nigel. 'Seeing Through Photographs', *Ratio* 1.1 (1998): 64-74 DOI: 10.1111/j.1467-9329.1988.tb00111.

Wetering, Ernst van de. *A Corpus of Rembrandt Paintings IV*, Dordrecht: Springer, 2005.

Wolf, Robert I. 'Advances in Phototherapy Training', *The Arts in Psychotherapy* 34 (2007): 124-133.

www.ingramcontent.com/pod-product-compliance
Lightning Source LLC
Chambersburg PA
CBHW052328220526
45472CB00001B/319